Praise for *Litera*

The power of language rests not just in *what* words are said, but in *how* they are said. The words of Scripture are no exception. Perhaps no tool is more useful, or more often overlooked, than a basic understanding of how the Bible speaks. Kristie offers excellent help to those who want to read the Bible as it is written: as a collection of different ways of writing, all telling one marvelous story.

JEN WILKIN, author and Bible teacher

Reading the Bible is important, but *how* we read it makes all the difference. Through a simple and concise approach, Kristie Anyabwile helps readers grasp the literary genres of the Bible. With plenty of aha moments to spare, this book helps us go to God's Word with fresh understanding, giving way to a true, rich, and robust study of the Scriptures.

EMILY JENSEN & LAURA WIFLER, cofounders of Risen Motherhood; coauthors of *Risen Motherhood: Gospel Hope for Everyday Moments*

Most of us know instinctually that we don't read poetry the same way we read historical narrative. And we don't read apocalyptic the same way we read discourse. But most of us need a little help in developing our skills for reading and understanding the types of literature in the Bible we're less familiar with. In this uncomplicated and insightful book, Kristie hands us some tools to use in the text that will help it to open up to us, so that we will become better able to understand and apply it to our lives.

NANCY GUTHRIE, author and Bible teacher

The most characteristic failing of preaching and Bible teaching today is the almost total lack of attention to the genres of the Bible. The customary approach to the Bible is to operate on the premise that every passage belongs to the same undifferentiated genre, understood to be a repository of ideas. Kristie Anyabwile knows that adequate analysis of the Bible requires close attention to its specific genres. Her book is an introduction to the major genres of the Bible, and she shows how an awareness of these genres can guide our encounter with a passage in the Bible. This book moves beyond accurate theory (information about the genres of the Bible) to practice, and a major strength of the book is that it contains an abundance of tips for reading and interpreting the Bible in light of its genres.

LELAND RYKEN, author and professor of English emeritus at Wheaton College

Studying the Bible's literary genres doesn't have to be boring. In *Literarily*, Kristie Anyabwile does a masterful job of interweaving Scripture and relatable pop culture to help make the complex topic of literary analysis in the Bible both fun and easy to understand. The more we understand the rich treasures to be mined in the Bible's stories, the deeper our faith and love for God will grow. Kristie's book offers both the tools and the guide for this much-needed excursion.

MICHELLE AMI REYES, Vice President, Asian American Christian Collaborative; Scholar in Residence, Hope Community Church; author, *Becoming All Things: How Small Changes Lead to Lasting Connections Across Cultures*

One area of Bible study that routinely gets overlooked is a study of genre. With warmth and an overflow wisdom, Kristie Anyabwile helps to fill this gap by introducing readers to the different categories of literature the biblical authors used to write Scripture. She accomplishes what most authors cannot, making complicated truths simple and accessible. This is a must-have resource for anyone who wants to better understand the metanarrative of Scripture and see the Bible as the beautiful piece of literature that it is!

ELIZABETH WOODSON, author and Bible teacher

This little volume is a great start to reading the Bible well. Written in a very accessible way, but with depth for experienced readers, Kristie has put together a fantastic handbook for digging into God's Word. It will be of great value to the church!

ROBERT S. KINNEY, Director of Ministries for the Charles Simeon Trust

I've been waiting for this book! Kristie has given us an accessible guide to studying the Bible genres, laying a framework for how we read and ask questions of the literature of the Bible. Her goal isn't only better knowledge but transformation as disciples through the Word. What a valuable tool! Buy a box of them and see the light bulbs come on in your small group, church, or class. I cannot wait to recommend it in my classes and events.

TAYLOR TURKINGTON, Director of BibleEquipping

This book will give you a confident start if you're new to reading the Bible. Kristie writes in an accessible way that anyone can understand and she does so winsomely. So much is packed in this one little book. It's worth your time.

COLLEEN J. MCFADDEN, Director of Women's Workshops for the Charles Simeon Trust

Literarily

How Understanding Bible Genres
Transforms Bible Study

KRISTIE ANYABWILE

MOODY PUBLISHERS
CHICAGO

Unless otherwise indicated, Scripture quotations are from the *ESV® Bible (The Holy Bible, English Standard Version®)*, Copyright © 2001 by Crossway, a publishing ministry of Good News Publishers. Used by permission. All rights reserved.

Scripture quotations marked CSB are taken from the Christian Standard Bible®, Copyright © 2017 by Holman Bible Publishers. Used by permission. Christian Standard Bible and CSB® are federally registered trademarks of Holman Bible Publishers.

Edited by Annette LaPlaca
Interior design, cover design, and cover illustration: Kelsey Fehlberg
Author photo: Ayanna Shepherd

All websites and phone numbers listed herein are accurate at the time of publication but may change in the future or cease to exist. The listing of website references and resources does not imply publisher endorsement of the site's entire contents. Groups and organizations are listed for informational purposes, and listing does not imply publisher endorsement of their activities.

Library of Congress Cataloging-in-Publication Data

Names: Anyabwile, Kristie, author.
Title: Literarily : how understanding Bible genres transforms Bible study / Kristie Anyabwile.
Description: Chicago : Moody Publishers, [2022] | Includes bibliographical references. | Summary: "A single approach doesn't do justice to the variety of genres that make up the Word of God. In Literarily, Kristie Anyabwile reveals the value of studying the Bible literarily-that is, according to the literary style presented in a particular book, chapter, or passage"-- Provided by publisher.
Identifiers: LCCN 2021051752 (print) | LCCN 2021051753 (ebook) | ISBN 9780802423993 (paperback) | ISBN 9780802499806 (ebook)
Subjects: LCSH: Bible--Hermeneutics. | Bible--Criticism, interpretation, etc. | BISAC: RELIGION / Biblical Studies / Bible Study Guides | RELIGION / Biblical Studies / History & Culture
Classification: LCC BS476 .A59 2022 (print) | LCC BS476 (ebook) | DDC 220.601--dc23/eng/20211117
LC record available at https://lccn.loc.gov/2021051752
LC ebook record available at https://lccn.loc.gov/2021051753

Originally delivered by fleets of horse-drawn wagons, the affordable paperbacks from D. L. Moody's publishing house resourced the church and served everyday people. Now, after more than 125 years of publishing and ministry, Moody Publishers' mission remains the same— even if our delivery systems have changed a bit. For more information on other books (and resources) created from a biblical perspective, go to www.moodypublishers.com or write to:

Moody Publishers
820 N. LaSalle Boulevard
Chicago, IL 60610

1 3 5 7 9 10 8 6 4 2

Printed in the United States of America

To the women of Anacostia River Church,
as we seek to be equipped for every good work.
2 Timothy 3:17

CONTENTS

TASTE
AND SEE

How sweet are your words to my taste,

sweeter than honey to my mouth!

PSALM 119:103

Let's face it. Studying the Bible can be difficult. As a new Christian, I knew I needed to study the Bible to learn about God and His ways and His purposes for humanity. I just didn't know how to get started. Should I open the Bible randomly and just start reading? Should I start with Genesis and read straight through? Should I work through a written Bible study or join a small group studying a book of the Bible? Should I pick a topic I'm interested in and look up verses related to that topic? Once I decided on an approach, the difficulty increased as I ran into so many words I didn't understand, people and nations that were new to me, and so many questions with no idea where to look for answers. Over the years, I purchased commentaries (others' interpretation

9

and explanation of Scripture) and lexicons (dictionaries of the Greek and Hebrew words found in the Bible) with the hopes of gaining greater insight into the riches of God's Word and solving some of my difficulties.

In my early years as a Christian, I relied heavily on pre-packaged studies and was quickly introduced to the idea of inductive Bible study. Inductive Bible study is a method that insists on careful observation of the text, asking questions and marking repeated words, themes, and contrasts; then making interpretations to gain meaning from the Scriptures through word studies and answering the observation questions; then applying the text to our personal lives by determining how we should live given what we learn. This method of study changed the way I interacted with the Scriptures, as it helped me formulate good questions from the text and seek out meaning for the original audience as a springboard for making proper applications of the Scriptures to my life. For years, not only did I employ this method in my personal devotions but also in teaching the Bible to others through one-on-one Bible studies and small groups.

However, in using a strict observation-interpretation-application inductive Bible study approach, I often was left with additional questions and thoughts that didn't seem to fit that method. I learned that the Bible contains different genres, or categories, of literature such as law, wisdom literature, history, prophetic writings, apocalyptic literature, and the Gospels. Those categories helped me to determine how to read each book, whether literally or figuratively, what to look for as I read (facts or symbolism or proverbial wisdom), and what tone or disposition the book was calling me to as I read. I recognized that within each genre there were stories, poems, and various kinds of speeches. However, these ideas never merged into a concrete method of study, but instead became more like disparate puzzle pieces lying on the table of my mind, and I had no idea of what the final picture was supposed to look like. Eventually, I was introduced to the Charles Simeon Trust, a Bible training ministry for pastors and Bible teachers. Through my training with that ministry, I learned that the text was forcing me to ask different kinds of questions depending on the genre or the type of writing within a specific text (poetry, speech, dialogue, story, prophecy, etc.). For example, if I read a poem, I needed to ask questions about the organization of the stanzas of the poem, or the imagery present in a passage. If I read a story, I needed to know who the main characters were, to identify the main conflict in the story and how it was resolved, and how the climax (point of highest tension) in the story contributed to how I interpreted the text. The puzzle pieces were slowly coming together, and a clearer picture formed in my mind regarding the importance of literary styles in inductive Bible study. What became clear is that the Bible is, in part, a literary work and there is great value in studying it literarily, according to the literary style presented in a particular book, chapter, or passage.

A genre (ZHAN-ruh) is an artistic category that groups things that share similar topics, types, forms, or styles. We often think of genres as they relate to books, music, movies, or art. Genres help to categorize information in at least three ways. They help to *organize* information. For example, paintings can be organized in a gallery by landscape art, portraits, still life, or historic era. Genres also help us *make sense* of information. So if you are listening to music, the meaning you come away with will often be shaped by its genre. I love country music, but country music can be a bit tricky because sometimes a song will have a title that signals one thing, but the content is quite different. Knowing that the songs "Take Me to Church" or "H.O.L.Y." are in the country genre and not gospel will help me make sense of the words as I listen. Finally, genres help us *know what to expect* from what we read. If you pick up a book of fantasy, you know to expect a complex fictional world with otherworldly creatures like dragons, the influence of myth and folklore, adventure, and heroism. Similarly, Bible genres help us organize the books of the Bible, make sense of how to read them, and know what to expect from each book. They also show and tell the message of the Bible through stories and speeches; they help us read the Scriptures both literally (such as when we are given commands to obey and truths to hold on to) and literarily (according to the literary makeup of the book, chapter, section of Scripture we're reading). Finally, genres provide guidance on structuring the text for study, whether as a plot, argument, letter, prayer, or poem—elements that inform the questions we ask of the text.

Working together, the biblical genres walk us through God's progressive revelation of Christ throughout redemptive history. God gives His *law* to lay down His expectations for His people. *Narratives* show us the lived experience of God's people through history and how His plan for humanity unfolds. The *prophets* speak God's word to His people calling them to repentance and faith, warning them of the consequences of their sin, and helping them learn what the future holds for them. *Poetry* recalls history through prayer and song and calls people to worship and remembrance. *Wisdom literature* teaches people the value and meaning of life through proverbial wisdom. The *Gospels* and *Acts* are generally narrative, but singularly focus on the life and teachings of Christ, the Savior whom all Old Testament history, prophets, and poets anticipate. *Epistles* are letters written to churches and individuals to instruct and logically clarify the teachings of Christ and how the church should live in light of the gospel. *Apocalyptic* literature is highly symbolic content focusing on what is referred to as the end times and shows us where history is headed and gives us glimpses of eternity.

There have been many books written about the Bible as literature. Many of them are geared toward the seminarian or pastor and can be daunting for someone just beginning to understand Bible genres. That's where this book comes in. We can deepen our understanding of what God intends to communicate through His Word by learning to study the Bible according to its literary genres. Whether you are new to Bible study in general or you have been studying the Bible for years, this study is intended to give you a new set of working utensils to put in your drawer of Bible literacy and provide a framework for reading and understanding a book or passage. Genre study is not a replacement for the inductive study method, but it provides additional categories for observing, interpreting, and applying the Word of God.

The Bible is a feast! We need to know the intention behind the various courses and the ingredients that make up each "dish" so we can enjoy a well-balanced, healthy meal every time we come to the text. We will talk about technique and use words like *study* a lot, but my prayer is that study and technique will ultimately help you experience richer fellowship with Christ our Savior, to taste and see that the Lord is good!

Part 1

THE BIBLE IS...

1

THE BIBLE IS . . .
An Epic Story

> "Think of what you have done and rejoice,
> for you have rid the land of a great evil."
> CHRISTOPHER PAOLINI, ERAGON

What kind of book is the Bible? Is it B.I.B.L.E. (Basic Instructions Before Leaving Earth)? Is it a recipe book showing you how to put a bunch of ingredients together resulting in a tasty treat? Is it a massive whodunit book that provides clues about a mysterious character or set of events you won't understand fully until you get to the end? Is it fact or fiction? Literal or figurative? Prose or poetry? Many people have attempted to distill what the Bible is through common analogies that all break down at some point. So we begin *Literarily* based on what God Himself says about His Word. The Bible is wholly true and fully reliable (John 17:17; 2 Timothy 3:16–17). It is inspired truth meant to clearly articulate who Christ is so that our hearts are transformed to know and love Him deeply and to live for Him fully.

The Bible is a message from God written in epic fashion as a collection of anthologies to chronicle the story of Jesus' redemption of sinners and His appeal for us to live considering His work on our behalf. An epic is a very long poem that tells a story. In an epic story, virtue drives the hero. He or she works to serve the greater good. We are drawn to our heroes' world. Their interests become our interests; their passions become our passions.

In the Eragon fantasy book series, a young boy named Eragon and his dragon, Saphira, embark on a mission to bring the entire world of Alagaesia out from under the evil influence of Galbatorix. The world of Alagaesia is comprised of various people groups—dwarves, elves, Urgals, dragons, and humans. Their cultures and interests are at odds with each other, but they are challenged to lay those differences aside to defeat the encroachment of Galbatorix. None of their cultures will survive if he is allowed to reign unchecked. Galbatorix has stolen what is most precious to these societies to amass unrivaled power for himself. It soon becomes clear that the fate of Alagaesia will rest on Eragon. Can he and Saphira find a way to defeat Galbatorix? Unbeknownst to Eragon, a powerful force has guided and helped him along his journey. It is only when his need is most desperate that he is made aware of the guidance of this force. Even then, Eragon used every worldly means in his attempt to destroy Galbatorix. In the end, it would not be through might that evil would be destroyed. Evil would finally be destroyed through a breaking of mind and spirit.[1]

Every epic good-versus-evil story, like *Eragon*, reminds me of the story of Scripture, the truest and most heroic and epic story that has ever been known. The Bible is one epic story, organized as an anthology. Traditionally, an epic is presented as a poem. The Bible is not a poem (though it has lots of poetry in it), but it contains many of the other elements of an epic. It's otherworldly, ancient, and heroic, with strong themes of bravery and overcoming great odds for the benefit of humanity. It focuses on overcoming intense trials in view of a glorious future. Though there are many stories and books and themes, and though it spans thousands of years, it's written by the finger of God, inspired by the Holy Spirit, and all about one person, the Lord Jesus, and how from Him and through Him, and to Him are all things. Jesus breaks into a world full of competing interests. For Christians, the interests of Jesus become our interests. His passion, to take the gospel to the whole world, becomes our passion. He is our ultimate hero who lived a perfect life, died to save humanity from our sins and the sinful influence of the world and Satan, rose three days after death to showcase His power over death and the resurrection life that exists for those who believe in Him, and left us the deposit of the Holy Spirit to guide and direct us to know Him and live for Him.

GOD SPEAKS

The Word tells us that "all Scripture is breathed out by God and profitable for teaching, for reproof, for correction, and for training in righteousness" (2 Timothy 3:16). The profitability of the Bible is based on its divine origin, not just that there's good information to pull from, but that it contains ultimate truth and absolute authority. God Himself breathed out the words into the hearts and minds of prophets, historians, pastors, apostles, and even prisoners! These messengers wrote, not by their own will, but by God's will as they were carried along by the Holy Spirit (2 Peter 1:21).

God makes His eternal power and divinity known through the things we see in creation, so that we must testify to a basic knowledge of God that helps us know He exists, He is powerful, and He is divine. However, this knowledge alone is a great start but not sufficient in leading us to salvation in Christ. This is why the Word of God is necessary. If we could only know God through creation and without the aid of His Word and the work of His Spirit, we would be left in our sins. The fullness of God's revelation of Himself is through the Word. God not only *shows* us that He exists, but He *tells* us! The God of the universe spoke the world into existence. He created light and sky and land and sea and vegetation and the sun and the moon and stars and all manner of creatures in land, sea, and sky. This culminated in calling forth humanity to be fruitful and to multiply and to fill and subdue and maintain dominion and stewardship over all His creation. Into this world, He called His Son Jesus to be born in the womb of a virgin, and to live more than thirty years in complete obedience to Him, before dying on a cross to atone for the sins of humanity. Christ is the Word who was with God from the beginning (John 1:1) and who is indeed God made flesh (John 1:14). Jesus Christ and the gospel He brings is the full and final Word of God to humanity.

As a kid, I loved Friday and Saturday night boxing matches. My dad and I would prepare for a big event by baking our favorite boxed, yellow cake mix with loads of chocolate icing, and covering the entire cake with pecan halves. We devoured big slices of the warm, gooey cake with a huge scoop of butter pecan ice cream while watching fighters work their way up the ranks to win all the world title belts in their weight class, in hopes of one day becoming the next "undisputed world champion" in boxing. I can mark my childhood by celebrating the victories of boxing greats like Muhammad Ali, Evander Holyfield, Marvin Hagler, and Roy Jones, Jr. An undisputed champion is without rival, fully accepted, undeniable. God's Word is also indisputable, eclipsing all other sacred writings. No other religious or secular text has ever come close to the Bible in its accuracy, trustworthiness, or its authority over all creation. Why is this? It's not because someone wrote the Bible, laid it beside other great works, and found it to be the best among equals. It's because the Bible is not a mere book. It is, in essence, without error and without rival because God breathed truth into hearts and minds, onto scrolls, and in ink through men as they were carried along by God's Spirit.

Think of all the things you've verbalized or thought you needed in the past twenty-four hours. Here are some of the things I've said I need today. I need a break. I need chocolate. I need time to myself. I need to stretch my legs. I need to figure out what we're going to eat for dinner. I need to pick up my son from soccer practice. I need to respond to a text message. I need a new pair of jeans to replace my ripped ones (although ripped jeans are in fashion so maybe I'll keep them). I need a massage. And it's only the middle of the afternoon! There's so much day left and so many more "needs" to come! God's Word meets our most pressing spiritual needs while He also promises to care for our physical (Matthew 6:30) and emotional needs (Isaiah 26:3). The Lord gives us what we need for our soul's satisfaction. His Word awakens us to His grace and mercy and offers us wisdom and joy and enlightenment. Through the Word of God, we are warned against sin, encouraged to be discerning, and shown the blessings of righteous and holy living as we await our eternal reward.

Any decent chef will tell you the most important tool in the kitchen is a good, sharp chef's knife. Believe it or not, a dull knife is more dangerous than a sharp one. It takes way more effort to use a dull knife. The knife is more likely to slip off the item being cut, creating a higher chance of injury. A sharp knife is precise. It cuts clean through flesh and bone. And so it is with God's Word. We're told in Hebrews 4 that "the word of God is living and active, sharper than any two-edged sword, piercing to the division of soul and of spirit, of joints and of marrow, and discerning the thoughts and intentions of the heart" (4:12). This verse comes at the end of a long section on Sabbath rest. We're told in verse 11 that we are to strive to enter God's rest, which is ours when we believe in Christ. We enter His rest when we cease from our strivings and self-effort and depend on Him for strength, wisdom, grace, and more. Rest does not mean inactivity. The Word is active. It works, but we rest. We rest in the finished work of Christ. We rest in His care. We rest in knowing God's Word probes and exposes every thought and intention of our hearts and is effective in accomplishing all His purposes in our lives.

GOD RULES

In an old episode of *Star Trek: The Next Generation*, one of the characters was an AI life form named Data. In one episode, Data decided to pursue a romantic relationship with a human colleague to explore human intimacy. His new girlfriend says to Data, "You give me so much. You spend time with me when I'm lonely. You encourage me when I'm down.

No man has ever been kinder to me." It's obvious she's developed feelings for him. However, Data's programming doesn't give him the capacity for romantic love. He decides to create a program with a specific "subroutine" devoted specifically to the development of this relationship.[2] Regardless of how hard he tried, Data's advances toward his new girlfriend could only be artificially contrived.

Data's attempts are nothing like a relationship with God. Though we can't see Him, God is not robotic in His relationships with His people. Yes, He rules creation and all life, but He does so out of an abundance of love. He's not programming ideals but pouring out His perfect love into our imperfect hearts, giving us the ability to receive His love by faith in the Lord Jesus. Nothing Data's love interest could do would elicit emotion from Data, but God rejoices over us with singing! God gives, loves, gets angry, and more—yet He rules over His beloved with grace and mercy. Therefore, we should believe and obey His Word as the fullest revelation of God to humanity. Jesus Himself says that all the Scriptures speak of Him—the Old Testament law, the prophetic books, the psalms—and all that Scripture says about Him must be fulfilled (Luke 24:27, 44), including His suffering, death, and resurrection.

The Baker Encyclopedia of the Bible describes *biblical authority* as the idea that the Bible is the Word of God and as such should be believed and obeyed. Our society resists and challenges the idea of authority. Many people's deep reaction is that "no one is the boss of me." Baker goes on to say that since the concept of authority is generally challenged in our society, it leaves us with the question, "Who has the power and right to require submission?"[3] God alone has this right. Too often in Christian circles, we have abandoned God's authority and the authority of His Word. Instead, we've delegated it to trusted pastors, theologians, and teachers, who themselves have abandoned God's authority and have set themselves up as the sole trusted ruler over God's people, misleading and deceiving many to such an extent that Christians lose the ability to discern and hear the voice of God. As a result, some believers can only hear the narrative handed down by human leaders rather than by God through His Word. Lord, help us! This must stop. God has given us His Word as our authority, so we have the responsibility to believe, obey, and submit ourselves, in the words of the old saints, to "what saith the Lord." The focus of this book is to help us understand the Bible literarily and while this literary understanding will serve as a guardrail to help us yield to the authority of God's Word, we must also take time to understand the Bible in its cultural and historical contexts as well. A literary approach helps with this because the literary features of the text will help us make appropriate historical and cultural connections. No one likes to be told what to do. At one point in Data's new relationship, he tests out human emotion. His girlfriend challenges his behavior and says he's behaving foolishly. He taps into his "anger," points at her, and says "You don't tell me how to behave. You're not my mother!" When someone tells us to do something we don't want to do, or to behave in ways that rub against our natural tendencies, or when instructions are unclear or undesirable, or when we feel we're already doing everything right yet we're still challenged to change, we can often respond like Data, pointing our finger defiantly at God. We can erroneously assume there must be something wrong with God rather than accept His authority and submit to it.

How do we know the Bible is our authority? God tells us so. "All Scripture is breathed out by God" (2 Timothy 3:16). It's through the Scriptures that we learn about Christ (John 5:39–48). The Scriptures bear witness about Christ, and it is through Christ that we have eternal life. In Christ, we live and move and exist (Acts 17:28). The Bible is our authority because it was breathed out by the God who made us in His image to reflect His glory in the earth.

At a recent conference for teen girls, I asked a young teen what she was learning at the conference. She told me she was learning about authority. She said, "I always thought authority was mean, so I thought God was mean. I learned that God's authority is based on love. He's not barking orders at me to obey because He is mean. He's in the tunnel with me, guiding me in love." Most people don't connect authority and love as well as this teen girl. They see authority as punitive. Jonathan Leeman, in his book *The Rule of Love*, says, "God is love, but God is also King. His authority is a gift; and his gift of authority to people, when used for its creational or redemptive purposes, is an action of love. . . . Good authority strengthens and grows. It nourishes and draws out."[4]

God's authority given to us in the Word does provide rules and guidelines for us. These rules are not rigid and intended to punish; rather, they are guides that tell us all we need to know, believe, and observe for salvation. On just about any holiday, weekend, or Friday night entertainment, families and friends gather to play games. It's customary when playing any game that you play by "house rules." There are general rules that everyone agrees are standard to the game, but in a particular household some aspects of the rules can be added or changed according to the rules of that house. So, in the card game of Spades, the highest cards in the deck, called trump cards, are all the spades and sometimes the Jokers. However, in my house, the two of diamonds is also a trump card, and the two of diamonds and the two of spades become the third and fourth highest cards in the game, after the Jokers. Of course, if you are not familiar with this set of house rules, playing will take some adjustment. Players might decide to revert back to the general rules in future games. This is not how rules work with God. There are no "house rules" subject to each person's discretion to adjust as they see fit. No, all of God's words are to be obeyed by all of God's people. He is the authority. He is the "house." God's rules guide us in knowing Him personally, understanding forgiveness of sin and the gift of salvation, living godly lives, and obeying Him. The unfolding of God's Word provides us with light and understanding (Psalm 119:130). This understanding comes to us through the work of the Holy Spirit. We cannot understand spiritual realities apart from the help of the Spirit (1 Corinthians 2:14). God Himself must reveal to us His Word in words and ways we can understand (Romans 1:19). Speaking the truth of His Word to us in story and letter and proverb and prophecy is one way the Lord helps us to understand supernatural realities and truths that would otherwise be lost on us.

GOD REVEALS

The Bible is for everyone. There are aspects of God's Word that pertain to every human no matter their relationship to God—for example, that we are made in His image, that we have dignity and worth, that we can see His invisible qualities in His creation. This is called *general revelation*. But there are aspects of God's character and work in the world and in our hearts that can only be understood by those who have repented and believed in Christ. This is called *special revelation.*

God reveals Himself to us in who He says He is, what He is like, and what He does. What makes God *God?* He is the Creator of all, perfect, infinite, eternal, all-knowing, all-wise, unchanging. "He is the living God, enduring forever. . . . He delivers and rescues; he works signs and wonders in heaven and on earth" (Daniel 6:26–27). In Deuteronomy 4:35, Moses declares, "The LORD is God; there is no other besides him." He reminds Israel that God revealed Himself to them in miraculous ways—they heard His voice, they saw His fire guiding them by night and His cloud directing them by day. He delivered them from their enemies and brought them to the land of their inheritance. He did all this so they would know that God is God—ruler, creator, sustainer, provider, deliverer. Therefore, their right response should be to love, obey, and trust Him.

God reveals Himself to us through nature. He made the sunshine and rain to fall on sinners and saints alike (Matthew 5:45). Even the animals and shrubs understand they were created by the hand of God (Job 12:7–10). We also know something of God through lives, human experience as His image bearers (Genesis 1:26–27). We are born, we breathe, we see and touch and move and smell and taste, not by anything we have done, not by force of will or skill, but because God has given us these capacities. We know from Psalm 19:1 that the heavens declare the glory of God and the skies proclaim His handiwork. But we, too, as created beings, declare the existence of God, the power of God, the divine nature of God (Romans 1:19–20). Because God has clearly communicated these aspects of His character to us, we have no excuse for not believing the truth about who He is. The Scriptures go on to say that though God clearly reveals Himself to us, we neither honor Him as God nor do we thank Him. Instead we suppress the truth and give honor not to God but to other created things. It's like having a fancy, comfy recliner in your home, but you go out to a junkyard and replace the recliner with a rickety, wooden, functioning electric chair. No one would knowingly make such a trade, but that's what happens spiritually when we exchange God's truth for the world's lies. He offers us life, but the world only offers death and destruction. Our belief in the truth should lead to actions that uphold the truth.

Our knowledge of God is restored when the Holy Spirit invades our hearts to give us the ability to respond to the gospel message in saving faith. Were it not for the Holy Spirit, wooing us and softening our hearts and opening our eyes, we would not be able to discern spiritual truth. The Scriptures teach us that "the natural person does not accept the things of the Spirit of God, for they are folly to him, and he is not able to understand them because they are spiritually discerned" (1 Corinthians 2:14). The only way we can have the mind of Christ that allows us to have a true knowledge of God—rooted in the person and work of Christ—is for God by His Spirit to move us to that understanding.

It is through Jesus that God most clearly shows us what He is like and what He requires of us. Each Gospel writer introduced Jesus in a unique way, similar but distinct. In Matthew 1:1, we read that Jesus is "the son of David, the son of Abraham." Mark 1:1 calls him "the Son of God." Luke stated that his gospel is a story of the things they had witnessed concerning Jesus (Luke 1:1). When the angel Gabriel visited Mary to tell her that she would have a son and name him Jesus, he said Jesus "will be called the Son of the Most High" (Luke 1:32) and that He would rule over a kingdom that will have no end (Luke 1:33). Luke echoed Mark's description of Jesus as the Son of God (Luke 1:35). The Gospel of John describes Jesus as the Word (1:1), the true light (1:5–8), the Word who became flesh (1:14), and the One who makes Him known to us (1:18).

All of Scripture, what was written and the ways it was written, seeks to make Jesus known to us. The Scriptures teach us that, as the Word made flesh, Jesus was fully God. His birth was predicted and proclaimed by the angels (Luke 1:31; 2:11). We learn that "He is the image of the invisible God, the firstborn of all creation" and that all things were created by Him (Colossians 1:15–16). The whole fullness of God is in Jesus (Colossians 2:9), and Jesus refers to Himself as the I AM who existed before Abraham (John 8:57–59). Both Jesus and God are referred to as Alpha and Omega, indicating they are indeed the same person (Revelation 1:8; 22:13). To avoid the confusion of those who might think there might be two gods, Jesus clearly states that He and the Father are one (John 10:30).

While Jesus is fully God, He is also fully man. He was born (Matthew 1:18, 25). He grew (Luke 2:40, 52). He had emotions (John 11:35; 12:27). He ate and slept and moved in the world as all human people do. He died. But what makes Jesus unique among humanity is that He never sinned. He lived a perfect life of obedience to God and was therefore able to be the perfect, blameless, unblemished sacrifice God required as a substitute for the sins of humanity. In His body,

He took upon Himself the sins of all humanity of all time so that if any repent of their sins and trust in Him, they will have eternal life.

At the end of the first book in the Eragon series, Eragon defeated a vicious adversary who had wreaked havoc on the world of Alagaesia. Weakened by the battle, Eragon received the assurance he needed to continue his journey to fully and finally free Alagaesia from every evil foe. A stranger appeared in his consciousness to guide him to his next set of battles. This helper told him, "You are greater than you know, Eragon. Think of what you have done and rejoice, for you have rid the land of a great evil. You have wrought a deed no one else could. Many are in your debt."[5]

By analogy, the epic story that the Bible is telling—from Genesis to Revelation—is the story of how God redeems the people He created by sending Jesus to be the Savior of the world. He did what no other human could do. He defeated our greatest foe, Satan, and guaranteed our victory over sin and death through His death and resurrection. We enter this epic by opening our Bibles, longing to listen to God speak to us through His Word, joyfully submitting ourselves to His rule, and fully trusting in God's revelation of Himself in the person of Jesus Christ.

THE BIBLE IS . . .
Meant to Transform Hearts

An awareness of genre should program our encounter with a text,
alerting us to what we can expect to find.

ESV LITERARY STUDY BIBLE

The Bible is true, and the stories are varied—tragic, funny, adventurous, heroic. The stories are meant to transform hearts and not merely to hold interest and entertain. We find the gospel message throughout God's Word where we can see how it transforms hearts, how transformed hearts are expected to live in the world, and the longing of transformed hearts for the appearance of Jesus, our blessed hope.

TRANSFORMING HEARTS

There is order to the Bible. Structured like an anthology, God's Word is a collection of writings by different people on a similar subject. It's comparable to an epic narrative since it's full of adventure and heroism, but the Bible is so much more.

The purpose of the Bible is not to tell a good story about a great man. Its purpose is to reveal the mystery of Christ to a fallen world so that those who read it would have their hearts transformed. A transformed heart is one that has embraced the gospel—the life, death, and resurrection of Christ as accomplished for their salvation.

The Bible is God speaking to humanity His infallible, authoritative, complete Word that is sufficient and effective for all those God has chosen to save through the gospel. The gospel is the power of God for salvation to all who would believe in Jesus as Savior and Lord. This is the highlight and theme of the whole Bible, transforming hearts as people repent of their sins and trust in Christ.

GENRE

In our early years of dating and marriage, my husband and I frequently spent hours perusing the aisles of record stores and CD stores. We spent most of our time in the jazz section but would venture over to R&B, gospel, blues, or even classical music. The more time we spent in the stores, the more we allowed ourselves to sample the variety of *genres* offered. A musical genre is a general category that helps to identify a type of artistic work. Typical musical genres include jazz, R&B, Christian hip hop (CHH), pop, or country. Of course there can be overlap (like deciding if Taylor Swift's music is country or pop.) As we scanned the aisles, my husband and I appreciated the uniqueness of the individual genres, and it gave us a greater appreciation for music as a whole. We felt free to explore genres formerly foreign to us, like zydeco or classical or go-go. We discovered that there are rhythms, instrumentation, and stylistic elements that characterize each genre. Recognizing those elements helped us identify, understand, and appreciate a musical piece.

Similarly, the Bible is meant to be understood according to its literary genre. We say "literary genre" because the Bible is an inspired work that uses conventional literary techniques to aid our understanding. For our study, we'll focus on the eight main literary genres found in Scripture.

Law

The law is also called Torah in Hebrew. Jesus referred to the Torah as "the law of Moses" (Luke 24:44). These are the books of Genesis, Exodus, Leviticus, Numbers, and Deuteronomy. These five books (called the *Pentateuch* in Greek) form a unit because they are the main Old Testament texts written by Moses to be handed down to Israel so they would remember God's mighty acts and His instructions for how to live as they entered the Promised Land.

Old Testament Narrative

The word *narrative* indicates storytelling. Old Testament historical narratives include the books in the Old Testament that chronicle the history of Israel: Joshua, Judges, Ruth, Samuel, Kings, Chronicles, Ezra, Nehemiah, and Esther. Almost half of the Bible comprises narrative.

Prophetic/Apocalyptic

Prophets are men or women sent by God to speak the words of God to the people of God. Although there are no prophetic books written by women, there were women who functioned as prophets in both the Old and New Testaments (see the account about Deborah found in Judges 4–5, and Anna who is mentioned as a prophetess in Luke 2:36–38). The prophetic books are designated based on their length as major (Isaiah, Jeremiah, Ezekiel) or minor (Lamentations, Hosea, Joel, Amos, Obadiah, Jonah, Micah, Nahum, Habakkuk, Zephaniah, Haggai, Zechariah, Malachi).

Both Daniel in the Old Testament and Revelation in the New Testament are considered apocalyptic books because they reveal God's coming judgment of people and nations in highly symbolic imagery and language. Apocalyptic literature peers ahead into the end of days, "the day of the Lord." Other books in both the Old and New Testaments contain some apocalyptic literature, but not enough to make the whole book considered apocalyptic in category.

Poetry/Wisdom

Psalms is a whole book of poetry and songs. Job is mostly poetry, but also is considered a book of wisdom. There are literary elements that undergird each of these designations, which make it a bit tricky to categorize. Other wisdom books include Proverbs, Ecclesiastes, and Song of Solomon.

Gospels and Acts

The four Gospels and Acts are historical narratives, primarily consisting of stories and speeches centered on the life and teachings of Jesus. The four Gospels are Matthew, Mark, Luke, and John. The book of Acts is a historical account that follows the development of the early church after Jesus' ascension, as the Spirit worked in the hearts of people to respond to His life, death, and resurrection.

Epistles

Epistles are letters, and make up more than 75 percent of the books in the New Testament. The letters written by the apostle Paul are called *Pauline epistles*. Paul wrote some of these letters to churches (Romans, 1 and 2 Corinthians, Galatians, Ephesians, Philippians, Colossians, 1 and 2 Thessalonians) and some specifically to pastors (1 and 2 Timothy, Titus). The prison letters were written while Paul was imprisoned (Colossians and Philemon). The other New Testament letters are called *general epistles*: Hebrews, James, 1 and 2 Peter, 1, 2, and 3 John, and Jude. They are not written to churches in specific cities and have various authors.

TYPES

Within each major genre are three main types of writing that make up the chapters and sections of each book of the Bible.

Stories

Stories include a plot, or storyline, that seeks to resolve some issue, problem, or question through character sketches and scenes. Some examples of various stories found in Scripture are historical narratives, hero stories, parables, and biographies.

Poetry

The second type of writing you will often find in Scripture is poetry. Believe it or not, poetry makes up about a third of the Bible's content. We don't often think about it or notice because Hebrew poetry doesn't follow common rhyme schemes and meter that we recognize in Western poetry. Poetry includes songs, prayers, laments, and acrostics. Many of the prophetic books contain large sections of poetic writing.

Speeches

The third type of writing we find within each genre is speeches. A speech is one-way communication in which a speaker is addressing a specific audience. Speeches often come in the form of sermons, letters, laws, or prayers.

UNFOLDING THE STORY
OF REDEMPTION

C. S. Lewis understands that reading the Bible as literature makes sense. He says, "Those who talk of reading the Bible "as literature" sometimes mean, I think, reading it without attending to the main thing it is about. . . . That seems to me to be nonsense. But there is a saner sense in which the Bible, since it is after all literature, cannot properly be read except as literature; and the different parts of it as the different sorts of literature they are."[1]

Lewis knows that the Bible is not merely a book of literature. But he also understands that one must take into account its literary forms when reading it. We take time to understand genres and types, to read the Bible literarily, in order to read and appreciate the Bible in the way God presented it to us, so we might know and love and worship Him as fully as humanly possible. We read the Bible as an inspired literary work from the mouth of God, moving in the hearts and minds of holy servants, led by the Holy Spirit, for the purpose of transforming hearts by unfolding God's great story of redemption.

Part 2

TRANSFORMING BIBLE STUDY

3

RULES, RULES, AND MORE RULES
(Law)

I can meditate on the law day and night
because it reveals to me what is pleasing to God.
R. C. SPROUL, "WHICH LAWS APPLY?"

If you watch a lot of Marvel movies, you'll discover that overarching all the individual movies is a bigger narrative that ties all the individual movies together. We discover what fans refer to as "Easter eggs" scattered throughout each movie. These Easter-egg hints form a thread helping us to see how the larger story develops. Many movie fans will rewatch the movies, sometimes in chronological order so they can find the Easter eggs and better understand the larger narrative. The more you watch the movies, the more Easter eggs you pick up, the more you can see how the individual movies connect to each other and how they fill in the larger storyline.

Just like the Easter eggs scattered throughout the Marvel movies, the individual stories and chapters of the Bible are carefully curated, progressively revealing greater aspects of who Christ really is and what He has accomplished for humanity. He's not Thanos, randomly finger-snapping humanity in some sort of ethnic cleansing. Jesus is our Savior, sovereignly and patiently restraining judgment on a world that deserves it because of our sin, so that some might be saved through repentance from sin and trust in Christ. As we read the law, or any other genre of Scripture, our task is to discover what Easter eggs are scattered about and how they contribute to the metanarrative (big story) of the Bible.

WHAT IS THE LAW?

We often think of the law in two ways. In the more general sense, the first five books of the Bible are referred to as the law. These five books are called the *Pentateuch* (PEN-tah-took), from two Greek words: *pente*, meaning "five," and *teuchos*, meaning "books." In the Jewish tradition, the Pentateuch is referred to as the *Torah* (a Hebrew word meaning "law" or "instruction"). More broadly, the law books are instructions, not merely rules. The opening pages of the Bible describe how God created a perfect place for God's people to live under His rule. Genesis highlights God's instructions to Adam and Eve in the garden, describing how He expected them to live in perfect communion with Him.

When Adam and Eve failed, God purposed to create a new nation from one man, Abram, and his wife, Sarai, who would live under His rule. This young nation, commonly referred to as "the children of Israel,"[1] grew but was taken captive by a ruthless ruler. God delivered them from their oppressors and guided them to the place of promise, where He would dwell with them as their God if they would love and obey Him. He set a leader before them, Moses, who would be His spokesperson before the people. Most of the Pentateuch, from the middle of the book of Exodus to Leviticus, Numbers, and Deuteronomy, contains the instructions, or laws, that God gave to the people through Moses as he led Israel out of captivity and into the promised land of Canaan. God expected His people to live distinct from the pagan nations around them, holy to the Lord, and worshiping only Him. These laws were for their wisdom and understanding in the sight of the peoples around them, and for them to also teach their children to learn to fear God and obey Him (Deuteronomy 4:6, 9–10).

Another way we think of law in the Bible is the Ten Commandments. These formed the centerpiece of the Old Testament moral instructions meant to guide God's people in how to love Him and one another well and how to live in joyful obedience to Him and joyful community with their neighbors.[2]

So we have the "law books" (Genesis, Exodus, Leviticus, Numbers, Deuteronomy) that chronicle the establishment of God's people, their early history, and journey to the Promised Land. And we have the "law" summarized in the Ten Commandments as instructions to govern how God's people live under His rule. Throughout the Pentateuch and the entire Bible, echoes of the Ten Commandments permeate and serve as reminders for the people about God's expectations. We don't get very far in Scripture before we realize that God's people were not very good at remembering and obeying.

THE SIGNIFICANCE OF THE LAW

The law teaches us that God has a standard, one we could never meet on our own, one that binds every heart to obedience. Whoever does not keep the entirety of the law is cursed (Galatians 3:10). So the law makes our inability bubble to the surface, showing us that no one can be justified by perfectly obeying the law. The law leaves us with a burning question: If no one can obey perfectly, then how can we be justified by God? The Bible teaches us that those who are counted righteous before God do so by faith in Christ, who "redeemed us from the curse of the law by becoming a curse for us (Galatians 3:11–13). So when we read the law, we keep in mind that it points us to Christ's once-for-all sacrifice for sin (Hebrews 10:12).

The laws presented in Scripture were handed down by God, in dialogue with Moses, who delivered them in a series of speeches to the people of Israel. These laws were ceremonial, civil, and moral in nature, but function as part of the larger story that chronicles the Israelites from their exodus from Egypt to their wandering in the desert (and eventually to the conquest of Jerusalem by Babylon, which will be covered in the history chapter). Why were all these laws written down for Israel and for us? Ligon Duncan explains,

> So why did the law need to be written down? To restrain sin. Therefore, it can't be the answer to the problem of sin. It's there because of the problem of sin, not as the final answer to the problem of sin. The final answer to the problem of sin is the gospel! It's the person and work of Jesus Christ, in His life and death and

resurrection on our behalf, and our embrace of that by faith. That's the good news that deals with sin.[3]

We need the law not only to show us the problem of sin but also to lead us to the only solution for our sin problem, the Lord Jesus Christ and the deliverance He promises for those who repent of their sins and trust in Him. The law is the first act in the story of redemption, the first "Easter egg" that puts the rest of the Bible in motion. God created all things for His glory and gave His law as the standard by which all humanity would be measured. Since Adam's and Eve's sin, we are both unwilling and unable to obey God perfectly, so we enter the world as law-breakers. The Old Testament system of offering sacrifices to consecrate oneself to God, to repent and receive atonement for sin, and to restore fellowship and peace with God all required a blood sacrifice. An unblemished animal would serve as a substitute to die in the place of the one who offered it, in the place of the one whose sins required it. When we study the law, we're getting a handle on the first big Easter egg that will shape the entirety of Israel's life as the people of God, as they constantly offered up sacrifices to God because of their sins. The law provides a picture of our own need for a substitute and points us to Christ as the once-for-all sacrifice for our sins (Hebrews 9:26–28). Our Bible study is enriched when we become familiar with the types of laws we see in Scripture, with how they instructed Israel's conduct and worship, and with how the laws relate to us today.

UNDERSTANDING
THE LAW LITERARILY

Often the law is sorted into three categories: moral law (truths that are timeless and guide our behavior), civil law (laws about governing people and laws that shape the legal system), and ceremonial laws (laws concerning holy days, especially to guide the priests in their duties). These categories help the Bible reader know which laws apply to us today (usually the moral ones because they are timeless) and which ones only applied to ancient Israel. However, if we believe that "all Scripture is breathed out by God and is profitable for teaching, for reproof, for correction, and for training in righteousness" (2 Timothy 3:16), then we must be able to make legitimate applications from the time of ancient Israel to our day and show how even obscure laws like "you shall not sow your field with two kinds of seed, nor shall you wear a garment of cloth made of two kinds of material" (Leviticus 19:19) might hold significance for us today. A law like this one makes it sound like a sin to wear a silk and cotton blend!

Careful reading of the law requires that we consider the purpose of the laws and determine how those purposes relate to our lives today. Obviously, not all the specifics of the Old Testament laws still apply to us. Nowadays, devout believers eat pork, wear clothes made of two types of fabric, don't consider women ceremonially unclean after childbirth, and refrain from forcing women to drink bitter, poisonous water to see if they cheated on their husbands. But even if we contemporary believers don't need to abide by each one of the detailed and specific laws given in the Pentateuch, those Old Testament laws are still as instructive for us today as they were for ancient

Israel—just not in the same way. So, in the verse that says don't mix fabrics, in our day we might consider how our spiritual holiness has practical implications for our day-to-day lives.

When we look at the content of the law, we will see some recurring themes we should pay attention to, such as God's sovereignty, holiness, and grace; the shape of worship; and how seriously God takes sin. The law shows us that God cares about every aspect of our lives, our bodies, our attitudes toward our family members and neighbors, our celebrations. God is not just handing down random laws to trip up His people. When we read laws about what Israel could eat and what they must refrain from eating, we learn that God is holy and requires His people to live holy lives. God does not want them to be like the nations around them who did not know or worship God. He wanted His people to stand out, set apart for Him. When we read about what would make Israel unclean, we learn that God requires purification for His people, from the inside out. From their inward attitudes to their outward behavior, the Israelites were to be a people marked by holiness so all the nations would know they worshiped the one true God (Leviticus 20:26). The people knew this was impossible for them to achieve on their own, so they needed the symbolic substitute that helped them anticipate and long for the Messiah who would come to make all things new, reverse the curse of the Fall, and restore humanity to a right relationship with God.

Where Israel was bound by the law to keep and do it (Deuteronomy 4:6), we are bound by the law of Christ, which frees us from the demands of the law because Christ has fulfilled the law on our behalf. His sacrifice was what the Old Testament sacrificial system pointed to. We now come to God not through ritualistic sacrifice and cleansing but through faith in Christ. Through faith in Christ we are made holy and set apart for God, we receive forgiveness of our sins, and we are made clean. Neither Israel nor we can obey God perfectly. Israel looked forward to the Messiah to fulfill God's promise to deliver and restore His people. We look back on what Christ has done to deliver us from the domain of darkness and to transfer us to the kingdom of His beloved Son (Colossians 1:13). For Israel and for us, the law points to Christ.

In studying the law, keep in mind the type of writing within a chapter or passage. The books of Genesis, Exodus, and Numbers contain a lot of stories that chronicle the lives of the people of Israel, while the books of Leviticus and Deuteronomy mostly contain speeches. Most often in law, the speeches are rules spoken by God to Moses ("the LORD spoke to Moses" appears seventy-nine times in the law) and then from Moses to the people. Speeches usually try to convince the audience of an argument the speaker is making. A topic or theme emerges that anchors the speech. Stories vary, but they tend to chronicle the wilderness journeys of Israel, the lives of the patriarchs (Abraham, Isaac, Jacob, and Joseph), or accounts of kings and kingdoms that Israel encountered. We will go into more depth regarding biblical stories (narratives) in the next chapter. We also want to consider the historical and literary context, remembering that "the law of Moses" (the Pentateuch or the Torah) was written for the audience of eager Israelites who were ready to step into the Promised Land. From Genesis to Numbers, Moses bears with them for forty years, and still neither he nor the first generation of Israelites step foot in the Promised Land. By the time we arrive at the fifth book, Deuteronomy, it's time for the next generation of Israelites to take the mantle and receive what their forefathers were denied because of their disobedience. Moses starts all over again, restating all they'd heard about, known, and seen as children, so that they could be ready to keep and do all that God required of them.

We also need to look for theological clues that relate our passage to other parts of Scripture, such as key doctrines that might be connected to our passage, and to ways the New Testament teachings might shed light on our passage. These theological clues help us determine the main idea presented in the passage so we can look for other places in Scripture where that idea is highlighted and even discover how Jesus embodies that theological principle. For example, when we read the purification laws in Leviticus 11–15, we can investigate why the Lord instituted these laws as our theological clue. Leviticus 11:44–45 suggests the *why*: "For I am the LORD your God. Consecrate yourselves therefore, and be holy, for I am holy. . . . For I am the LORD who brought you up out of the land of Egypt to be your God. You shall therefore be holy, for I am holy."

From that clue *Be holy*, we can expand our study to consider how holiness is emphasized in other parts of Scripture, starting in Genesis, where God demonstrates His holiness by creating the world and everything in it. He is unique from all creation. He existed before time. He created and sustains all things by the power of His word. We can slowly walk through the Bible, noting the ways God illustrates His holiness (Exodus 3:5; Isaiah 6:3; Revelation 15:4) and the ways He calls His people to be holy as He is (Ephesians 1:4; Hebrews 12:14; 1 Peter 1:15–16). A great resource for learning more about holiness throughout the Scriptures is the cross references in your Bible, the little notes connected to a word or verse that take us to other places in Scripture that contain the same word or idea. Just remember that cross references point out similar words or verses without much context, so consider a cross reference carefully to see if it connects to your passage. You might also use a Bible app or online Bible to search for a phrase such as *Be holy*. As you make notes about holiness across Scripture, prayerfully discern what the Lord might be teaching Israel through the cleanliness laws. Leviticus especially leads us to understand that nothing unclean can come before a holy God. Sacrifices and offerings made in the temple required cleanliness. If a person had contact with something or someone unclean, a time of separation and purification had to take place, along with a blood offering brought to the priest to make atonement.

From following the clue about being holy to considering God's holiness and expectations of cleanliness across Scripture, turn your attention then to Jesus. Consider how Jesus teaches or embodies the idea of holiness and what it might mean for believers to think about the "clean and unclean" passages, considering what we learn about Jesus. Mark 1:40–44 tells how Jesus encounters a leper. A leprous person was required to live alone outside the camp, and no one was supposed to come in contact with him (Leviticus 13:45–46). Jesus heals the leper and directs him to go to the priest for proof so that the man could make the proper offering to God for his cleansing. Jesus demonstrates His divinity by doing what only God could do—touch an unclean person and not become unclean Himself, and heal infectious disease by the power of His word.

We noted the holiness clue, considered it across Scripture,

and focused our attention on Christ's holiness, so now we are ready to consider our contemporary context and try to determine how the theological principle we're discovering in the law (in this case, holiness) can be worked out in our lives, how we fall short, what we need to avoid or to cling to, ways we might understand Christ's example and teaching, and how we can both love God and our neighbor with that theological principle in mind.

Many readers rush through or ignore parts of the law because they find it tedious and uninteresting—just a bunch of old rules that are hard to connect with the other parts of the Bible or with our lives today. The law transforms Bible study by helping us see how the law provides instructions for God's people that call them to faithfulness that reflects God's holiness and humanity's sin, restrains evil, and reveals Christ and His rule over our lives.

TRANSFORM YOUR STUDY OF LAW

Work through the process of studying an Old Testament law.

1. Read Deuteronomy 10:12–22.

2. Decide if the passage is a speech or story.

3. Read Deuteronomy 1:1–46 and 3:18–29. What is happening with God's people at this time?

4. What is the main theme that runs through this passage? What is God requiring of His people?

5. Look for the theological clue by asking why God is making such requirements of Israel.

6. What other places in Scripture capture the main principle from this verse? Feel free to use the cross references in your Bible or do a key word search in your Bible app or online Bible.

7. How does Jesus teach or embody this principle?

8. How might you walk out this principle in your life? Be specific.

4

THIS IS A STORY ALL ABOUT HOW . . .
(Old Testament Narrative)

Stories don't tell the truth confrontationally. They don't coerce you.
They don't argue with you to believe them. They just are. The power
of the story isn't in summing it up, drilling it down, or reducing it to
an abstract idea. The power of the story isn't in the lesson. The power
of the story is the story.

SALLY LLOYD-JONES, "WHAT STORIES DO"[1]

Everybody likes a good story, especially an engaging story with unexpected twists and turns. Stories captivate, explain, reveal. They evoke strong emotions and sometimes transport us into the past or future, to land or sky or sea, or even to imaginary and fantastical worlds that feel as if they really do exist. Stories, real or imagined, affect us. A really good story will engage the intellect and emotions. They transport us to places and circumstances that sometimes echo or mirror our own experiences, and even if the people, places, and perspectives are new to us, they tap into a part of our common human experiences of love, loss, and longing.

In the sitcom *The Fresh Prince of Bel-Air*, the theme song summarizes the plot of the entire series. The song begins "This is a story all about how, my life got flipped, turned upside down."[2] The rest of the song tells us the background of the main character, how he ended up living with his uncle and aunt in ritsy Bel Air, and sets the audience's expectations that this story will center around the clash of cultures.

I love the opening line because every good story is a story of "how"—how people lived, loved, lost, taking us on the journey with them that we might learn from their experiences.

WHAT IS OLD TESTAMENT NARRATIVE?

Biblical history, also called Bible narratives, is history told in story form. These stories tell the history of God's people from the beginning of the world, to when God's people were held in captivity (exile) in Babylon, to the time after the exile (postexilic), to the time of Christ, to the rise of the church, to the consummation (the end of history and fulfillment of God's promises to His people). This type of history makes up almost half of the Bible. Narrative, historical literature can be found throughout most Old Testament books, but the books of Genesis, Exodus, Joshua, Judges, Ruth, 1 and 2 Samuel, 1 and 2 Kings, 1 and 2 Chronicles, Ezra, Nehemiah, and Esther are Old Testament narratives that specifically chronicle the history of God's people before Christ's birth.

These narratives move the overarching story of the Bible forward from God's call to Adam and Eve to be fruitful and multiply and fill the earth (Genesis 1:28), to His warning against disobedience (2:16–17), to His law outlining His expectations of His people to love and obey Him in a fallen world, to the unfolding story that helps us see the ways God's people responded to His instructions and the consequences of their actions. These stories explain the past by setting us in a specific place and time, introducing us to the problems various historical characters faced and how those problems were solved, and helping us to see how we are to live in light of the characters' successes and failures. Narratives showcase embodied, imperfect human experience as both a mirror and a window—a mirror that helps us to see our lives reflected in the lives of those in Scripture, and a window through which we can see the lives and circumstances of others and learn from them. There are narratives in the New Testament as well; however, the uniqueness of the gospel narratives and their recorded history will be treated in a separate chapter.

Narrative stories convey meaning through character interactions and development, conflict resolution, problem solving, and emotional release. Through these narratives we see real-life situations that highlight themes of power and vulnerability, strength and weakness, victory and failure, hiding and exposure, loss and gain, mystery and revelation, virtues and vices, poverty and wealth, perseverance and acquiescence, joy and pain, sunshine and rain.[3]

If we're paying close attention, any story can teach us moral lessons about God and ourselves, but the uniqueness of biblical narratives is that they are intended by God to help us understand His ways with humanity and how we might live as His people by learning from the foils and faith of the biblical characters living under His sovereign rule.

UNDERSTANDING NARRATIVES LITERARILY BY FOLLOWING THE PLOT

The beauty of narratives is that they show rather than tell. The storyline (also called the plot) helps us discover what the story is emphasizing so we avoid improperly spiritualizing (looking for deeper spiritual meaning beyond what the text and context allow) or blindly contextualizing the narrative (bringing the text forward to our day too quickly). A narrative is meant to be engaging and memorable, yet its meaning should be fairly easy to grasp. Narratives add the drama, the comedic relief, the intense ebbs and flows of emotion that keep us on our toes as we read. These are the page-turners of the Bible and help us to understand the nature of humanity and how we reflect or discredit God's character.

Narratives center around the plot. The plot is the whole of the story from beginning to end and generally follows an organized and unified path that gives shape to the story. This path is often referred to as a plot arc. The plot arc has a beginning, middle, and end. The beginning of the plot consists of *characters* who are usually placed within a particular setting and an *inciting incident* that sets the main action of the story in motion, often creating tension or a problem that needs to be solved or a question that needs an answer. The middle of a plot is the nail-biting part of the story, called the *climax,* where the reader is on edge waiting to see how the problem will be solved. At the end of the plot is the *resolution*, in which a new normal is established and the setting for a new plot is initiated.

Setting

The setting is sort of like a cake plate. Its primary job is to hold the cake. It's the foundation on which the cake is decorated and showcased. You want it to look appealing, but only to the extent that it draws the eye to what's on it, the cake itself. Similarly, the setting of a narrative is foundational. Everything in a story takes place in a context—that is, at a certain time and place in history and under specific circumstances. The setting is not usually the main point of a narrative, but it is necessary because it holds all the details of the story, drawing you in so you can begin to see the story's shape. Often characters are introduced within the setting that provide additional historical and cultural context and give us a clue as to who might be involved in the inciting incident. This is important for biblical narratives because the movements of God and the characters' character are keys to understanding the purpose for which the narrative is written.

Take, for example, the opening verses of the book of Esther: "Now in the days of Ahasuerus, the Ahasuerus who reigned from India to Ethiopia over 127 provinces, in those days when King Ahasuerus sat on his royal throne in Susa, the citadel, in the third year of his reign he gave a feast for all his officials and servants" (Esther 1:1-3). The setting is "in the days of Ahasuerus" (ah-HAHS-veh-ruhsh).[4] A quick search in a study Bible or Bible dictionary will help us determine that the third year of his reign would have been around 483 BC since Ahasuerus ruled from 486 BC to 465 BC.[5] During this time, the king held a feast for 180 days to show off his riches and the greatness of his power (1:4), and at the end of this time he held a seven-day feast for those in his palace during which people could eat and drink as they desired (1:8).

His queen, Vashti, also held a feast during this time (1:9). Even though the title of the book suggests that Esther is its key character, she has not been mentioned yet. Instead, the setting emphasizes the activity of the king. We learn that his banquets were lavish (1:7) and limitless (1:8). We are not told directly, but, given the grand gestures of the king, we get the impression that he was quite showy. The setting also introduces Queen Vashti (1:9), whose actions will be important as we move into the next aspect of the plot.

Inciting Incident

The inciting incident initiates the main action of the plot, exposes the purpose for the narrative, and culminates with the climax. Depending on what type of story is being told (hero story, suspense, test, poetic justice, foreshadowing), the inciting incident brings us closer to the heart of the story and helps us know what the story is about, telling us who is doing what and why. It connects us to the characters and helps us journey with them through the narrative. The story continues to build throughout the inciting incident and the action rises because the main character's trajectory or world is upset in some way.

Here's the inciting incident in the story of Esther:

> *On the seventh day, when the heart of the king was merry with wine, he commanded . . . the seven eunuchs who served in the presence of King Ahasuerus, to bring Queen Vashti before the king with her royal crown, in order to show the peoples and the princes her beauty, for she was lovely to look at. But Queen Vashti refused to come at the king's command delivered by the eunuchs. At this the king became enraged, and his anger burned within him. (Esther 1:10–12)*

In this opening story, the inciting incident is the king's command to his officials and Vashti's refusal. The king commands his queen to parade herself before his friends (a rude request, to say the least) and she refuses (no one refuses the king). He's already paraded his riches, his fine linen, gold couches, precious stones, his royal wine, and all that he owned. Given his behavior thus far, of course he would want to parade his beautiful queen before his guests. It's classic narcissistic behavior. But Vashti would not have it. None of her words are recorded here. We are just told by the narrator that "Vashti refused to come," and that's all we need to add intrigue and a little trepidation that leads to the next aspect of the plot.

Climax

The climax of a narrative will center around a question that needs an answer, a prediction or foreshadowing of something yet to be fulfilled, what will happen next or how something will turn out, whether or not the main character passed a test, if someone got what they deserved, or if there was an unexpected outcome or reversal of expectation. In the Esther narrative, the king's response is clear: "Then the king said to the wise men who knew the times . . . 'According to the law, what is to be done to Queen Vashti, because she has not performed the command of King Ahasuerus delivered by the eunuchs?'" (Esther 1:13, 15).

Oh snap! What's gonna happen next?! Apparently nothing like this had ever happened before because even the king had to consult his wise men to determine what should be done to the queen for disobeying his direct command. The gravity of her refusal is detailed in verses 16–18, revealing that her disobedience was not only seen as against the king, but against everyone—nobility and commoners, men and women—in the entire kingdom. Her refusal had upset the status quo and was feared that it would dismantle families and cause "contempt and wrath in plenty" (1:18). This is the highest point of tension in this story so far. It's the point at which there's a lingering question that must be answered to move the plot forward and to relieve the tension. This is the "cut to commercial" part of the story where you're left in limbo until you've been convinced that only one brand of tissue is the "quicker picker upper." So what happens to Queen Vashti, and how is the societal norm maintained or smashed in the story?

Resolution

There's a lot we can say about how things are resolved in this story. Is it a nice, happy ending? Well, not for Queen Vashti. Here's how this story from Esther chapter one resolves: "If it please the king, let a royal order go out from him . . . that Vashti is never again to come before King Ahasuerus. And let the king give her royal position to another who is better than she. So when the decree made by the king is proclaimed throughout all his kingdom, for it is vast, all women will give honor to their husbands, high and low alike" (Esther 1:19–20).

Vashti is removed from her position and banned from ever appearing before the king again. Though banished, we see her as the strongest character in the story. In literature, Vashti is considered a foil, a character whose actions and intentions draw your attention to another character in the story. In this story, Vashti's fortitude stands in contrast to the fragility of the king and the men who cater to him. She may also serve as a foil to Esther in some ways, but that's a story for another day. The resolution in this story is also not a pleasant one for the people of the kingdom, whose leaders use the rule of law they have created to accommodate the insecurities of weak men and promote the silencing of women.[6] It's not a happy ending, but the tension of what would happen to Vashti is resolved and things are put in motion for a new normal. Letters were sent throughout the royal provinces in the language of every people group so that all men would "be master in his own household" (1:22). Knowing that Esther is soon to step on the scene, we begin to see the makings of a new plot as we wonder what new woman the king will choose as his queen and how the people will respond to this new edict.

As the full plot is revealed, we see God at work through human experiences and we see how people relate and respond to Him. We see humanity's fallen nature and sin but also our capacity for genuine faith and obedience. In this account of Queen Vashti contrasted with King Ahasuerus, we see another contrast. The vanity of King Ahasuerus, whose exertion of power revealed his true nature as a weak earthly king, provides a marked contrast to Christ's humility, which revealed His true nature as King of kings. King Ahasuerus used his power and riches to boost his own pride and to suppress and silence his subjects. Christ laid aside His power and riches to come to earth as a humble servant to redeem a people who would curse and mock Him. The constrasts starkly demonstrate the difference between true strength and weakness, and we leave this story longing for a righteous king.

Not every biblical narrative neatly follows the plot arc, but since stories make up the majority of narratives and much of the Bible as a whole, we have focused our time on the plot arc. However, there are other ways to describe the movements in a passage, such as following time references that serve to chronicle history, analyzing character behaviors and finding the main foil to compare and contrast with the main character, or identifying the main scenes within a passage and discerning how those scenes carry the plot forward.

TRANSFORM YOUR STUDY OF NARRATIVES

The plot must hold together so that the sequence of events makes sense as a unit. The goal of using the literary technique of a plot arc in studying biblical narratives is so we might move beyond reading narratives as individual, self-contained stories with moral lessons on good versus evil and do's and don'ts. Rather, we want to see how each individual story contributes to what God is doing throughout history to redeem a people for Himself, to view human experiences in ways that point us to our need for Christ, and to connect each narrative to the story of the Bible as a whole (the metanarrative).

Study 1 Samuel 4:1–11, working through the plot arc. Though this passage is set within a larger plot that concludes in 7:1, this passage does have a distinct plot arc.

1. Consider the context from chapters 2 and 3, and 4:12–7:2. What is happening with God's people at this time?

2. Who are the main characters (individuals and groups) in chapter 4:1–11? What do you learn about them? Consider the literary context from chapters 2 and 3.

3. Find the plot arc of the passage by identifying the setting, inciting incident, climax, and resolution.

4. Make note of any themes of power/vulnerability, strength/weakness, victory/failure, etc.

5. What do you learn of God and His ways in this passage? What attributes of God come to mind?

6. How might this passage encourage us, warn us, or challenge our thinking and behavior?

7. How does Christ embody the biblical principle from this narrative?

8. How might your life be influenced in light of what you learn from this passage?

5

PRAYERS AND SONGS
(Poetry)

I know a funny little man,
As quiet as a mouse,
Who does the mischief that is done
In everybody's house!
There's no one ever sees his face,
And yet we all agree
That every plate we break was cracked
By Mr. Nobody.
ANONYMOUS[1]

This poem is one we love to recite in our home, not only because it accurately describes our conversations when things go missing or awry, but also because it's such a catchy, rhythmic poem. It's a sing-songy one you don't have to work hard to memorize. It kind of flows. We can all relate to Mr. Nobody. We remember those instances when the beautifully decorated cake has a toddler-sized finger swipe, and when the question was asked, "Who swiped frosting from the cake?" or "Who left the toilet seat up?" or "Who drank the last of the orange juice and left a tiny corner in the bottle in the fridge?" Nobody answered, so Nobody must have done it. This kind of poem is funny and memorable and relatable. So why is it that people often experience a disconnect with poetry? Well, not all poems are funny. Some are downright sad. One of the saddest poems I can remember was introduced to my fourth-grade class by our teacher, Mr. Milligan. He recited it to us one day in class, and everyone was in tears by the time he finished. This is how the poem, "Rags," begins:

> We called him "Rags." He was just a cur,
> But twice, on the Western Line,
> That little old bunch of faithful fur
> Had offered his life for mine.
>
> And all that he got was bones and bread,
> Or the leavings of soldier grub,
> But he'd give his heart for a pat on the head,
> Or a friendly tickle and rub.[2]

The main character was an endearing dog, who fought alongside soldiers in WWI. The imagery captured his sweet spirit and devotion and courage, and the dramatic surprise at the end was too much for our ten-year-old hearts and minds. That poem accomplished what good poetry should. It engaged our imaginations and our emotions with brevity, depth, and lyricism. By *lyricism* I mean that the poem has an expressive, engaging, almost musical style that adds structure, beauty, and movement in the poem. I'd commend it to you with tissues in hand.

In the English-speaking world, whether they rhyme or not, poems have a lyrical style, from alternating rhyme schemes, to limericks, to haikus, to sonnets. Alternating rhyme schemes have a set pattern of lines that rhyme, usually every other line or each couplet (two lines) of a poem. A limerick is usually funny and has five lines, with the first, second, and last lines rhyming and lines three and four rhyming. A haiku doesn't rhyme. It contains three lines with a set pattern of syllables that provide its lyrical quality. Lines one and three have five syllables and line two has seven syllables. A sonnet is a poem of fourteen lines with ten syllables in each line, usually written with every second syllable stressed (iambic pentameter), like this: "This BOOK is GOOD, but I must GET some SLEEP."

While there are some similarities between modern English poetry and biblical poetry, such as communicating big ideas with brevity and beauty, as well as engaging the imagination and emotions, there are some unique features of biblical poetry that will help us as we study the poetic books of the Bible.

WHAT IS BIBLICAL POETRY?

Poetry makes up about thirty percent of the Bible. Biblical poetry is image-heavy biblical writings, with discernible parallel lines that convey meaning concisely through figurative language and emotional intrigue. Biblical poetry can come in the form of songs, prayers, or liturgical readings (prayers or songs for worship). It follows the Hebrew tradition, which is not based on rhyme schemes and lyricism. Its structure, beauty, and movement are marked by parallelism (two or three, or sometimes four, parallel lines of verse that form a unit), and by imagery (word pictures that succinctly capture the life and actions of people).

We are most familiar with the Psalms as a book of poetry, but other books such as Proverbs, Job, Lamentations, and the Song of Solomon are also primarily poetry. Many of the prophetic books are entirely poetic (most of the minor prophets—Hosea, Joel, Amos, etc.) or contain significant sections of poetry (such as Isaiah or Jeremiah). Poetry was the medium the prophets used most often to communicate God's Word to His people because the Bible was orally communicated before it was written down. It was written for the ears. Just as the plot drives a narrative story so that it can be retold with a great degree of accuracy and drama, poetry is for memorization and recitation, to recall the acts of God and the lives of God's people in a creative and succinct way. Biblical poetry is meant to be *used*, to be prayed or sung, or acted upon in worship. Poetry makes difficult concepts accessible, long historical accounts concise, warnings piercing, blessings beautiful, and prayers and liturgies worshipful.

ORGANIZATION OF THE PSALMS

Since the majority of poetic literature is found in the psalms, it will be helpful to understand some key features often found in the psalms. First, the psalms are the praise songs of the people of God. About half of them were written by David. We know this because they contain inscriptions that say, "A psalm of David," sometimes adding a bit more description of the occasion in which he wrote it (see Psalms 34 or 52, for example). There are a handful of additional named authors of various psalms, and several with no authors named at all.

The opening inscription also sometimes provides musical instructions for the choirmaster, or it indicates that the psalm is a prayer (Psalm 90) or a song of thanksgiving (Psalm 100).

Second, the psalms are organized into five books. Before each new book, the previous one ends with a verse that says something like "Blessed be the LORD" or "Blessed be the LORD, the God of Israel" (see Psalms 41:13; 72:18; 89:52; 106:48). Some believe that the five books correspond to the Pentateuch, providing memorable recitations that survey the history of Israel in a songbook of sorts, as they move from themes of sin and lament and judgment to redemption and thanksgiving and praise.

Third, the psalms can be categorized according to various literary types that help us understand the purpose of the psalm and provide insight into how we understand it. Psalms of lament (Psalms 3, 13, 69) were written, according to one pastor, "*by* hurting people *for* hurting people," calling them to acknowledge the sin and brokenness of the world and to pray in faith for deliverance.[3] Wisdom psalms (Psalms 1, 37) provide direction and guidance for God's people. Royal psalms (Psalms 21, 110) anticipate the messianic kingship of Christ. Praise psalms (Psalms 8, 150) center on God's character and the rightful response of His worshipers. Imprecatory psalms (Psalms 7, 58) call on God to pour out judgment and justice on His and the people's enemies. Thanksgiving psalms (Psalms 29, 136) offer gratitude to God for answered prayer, for His goodness, and for His abundant blessings. There are other categories, some of which are evident from the psalm itself, either in the inscription at the beginning or in the body of the psalm. It's helpful to ask as you read the psalms, "What type of psalm am I reading, and what is it revealing to me about God?"

UNDERSTANDING POETRY LITERARILY

C. S. Lewis captures the significance of reading biblical poetry literarily:

> Most emphatically the Psalms must be read as poems; as lyrics, with all the licences and all the formalities, the hyperboles, the emotional rather than logical connections, which are proper to lyric poetry. They must be read as poems if they are to be understood; no less than French must be read as French or English as English. Otherwise we shall miss what is in them and think we see what is not.[4]

We do not want to miss what is in biblical poetry, nor do we want to think we see something that is not there. To understand biblical poetry, we must identify the features that typify the genre and that help us see what is there. Some of the following terminology may be new from what you are accustomed to in analyzing poetry, but that's because most of the terms used here are Greek in origin, whereas the poetic terminology we are most familiar with is borrowed from French or Italian or Latin. First, we need to know that biblical poetry is made up of units of thought, a line, called a colon. These *cola* (plural) come in pairs most often but can also contain between one and four parts to make up a line. A group of lines that share one theme is called a strophe (STROH-fee). When a poem contains several strophes that share one theme, it is called a stanza.[5] Whew! That's a lot. Let's take the first two verses of Psalm 24 as an example to see these parts at work.

> *¹The earth is the LORD's and the fullness thereof,*
>   *the world and those who dwell therein,*
> *²for he has founded it upon the seas*
>   *and established it upon the rivers.*

One line is a cola, so two lines are *bi*colon. You can see that verse one is a bicolon, and so is verse two. Together, these verses make up the first strophe of the psalm. A strophe functions like a paragraph. You may hear some people refer to a strophe as a stanza, but we won't quibble with them because in English poetry, stanza is the term we use to designate paragraph-like divisions in a poem.

PARALLELISM

The Bible was not originally written with verse numbers, punctuation, or line breaks, so how do we know where the line breaks are? If you look closely at the first verse, we notice that there is a repetition of the idea that the world and everything in it belongs to the Lord. There is a *parallel* idea being communicated. In parallelism, the lines are related to each other in some way. Most often, the second line repeats or mirrors the first line (synonymous parallelism). Other times, the second line may contrast (antithetical parallelism), compare (emblematic parallelism), complete (synthetic parallelism), or extend (staircase parallelism) the thought of the first line.[6] At the beginning of verse two, we see the connecting word *for*, which lets us know we are about to be given the reason for why the earth and everything in it belongs to the Lord. The reason is that He created it all! We can't help but recall Genesis 1 where we're told the creation story, that "in the beginning, God created the heavens and the earth" (Genesis 1:1), that He gathered the seas together in one place and called up the dry land (1:9) and populated the seas with living creatures (1:20, 22).

Psalm 24:1–2 points to God's sovereign rule and power over all creation. As we observe how the parallel lines fit together, we begin to grasp the value of parallelism in our study of God's Word. The primary goal in identifying parallelism in biblical poetry is so we can see, feel, and hear what is being emphasized in a set of verses. In Psalm 24:1–2, we are called to *see* that everything in creation belongs to the Lord, to *feel* the weight of God's power and sovereignty over all things and our smallness in relation to His grandeur, and to *hear* the call to place ourselves under His rule.

STROPHES AND STANZAS

As we continue our look at Psalm 24, verse three opens in a clear shift from the previous verses. This shift helps us to see a new strophe starting:

> *³ Who shall ascend the hill of the* Lord*?*
> *And who shall stand in his holy place?*
> *⁴He who has clean hands and a pure heart,*
> *who does not lift up his soul to what is false*
> *and does not swear deceitfully.*
> *⁵He will receive blessing from the* Lord
> *and righteousness from the God of his salvation.*
> *⁶ Such is the generation of those who seek him,*
> *who seek the face of the God of Jacob. Selah*

The psalmist David asks, "Who shall ascend the hill of the

LORD? And who shall stand in His holy place?"This question flows naturally from the knowledge of God as sovereign Creator. If that is who He is, who can come into His presence? Who can stand before Him? He is holy and where He dwells is holy, so those who come before Him in worship must be holy too. But what does that look like? Where verses one and two center on the character of God, this strophe focuses on the character of the worshipers. Notice the repetition of their innocence (clean hands, pure heart) and integrity (does not speak falsely or deceitfully). What binds these verses together is the idea that God is holy and so His people who enter His presence must also be holy. That holiness forms the unifying theme of Psalm 24:1–6.

IMAGERY

The second half of the psalm starts a new stanza because we move away from the theme of God as holy toward the theme of God as victor:

> *7Lift up your heads, O gates!*
> *And be lifted up, O ancient doors,*
> *that the King of glory may come in.*
> *8Who is this King of glory?*
> *The LORD, strong and mighty,*
> *the LORD, mighty in battle!*
> *9Lift up your heads, O gates!*
> *And lift them up, O ancient doors,*
> *that the King of glory may come in.*
> *10Who is this King of glory?*
> *The LORD of hosts,*
> *he is the King of glory! Selah*

The gates are given the human characteristic of a *head* that is lifted. The doors are *ancient*. The image of the king is of a *mighty warrior*. The tone carries urgency and a rising crescendo as the voices inside the gate inquire, "Who is this King of glory?" Imagery is an important element in poetry. Imagery is the use of descriptions of people, places, objects, and ideas to stir our imaginations, our senses, and our emotions. Imagery is a large part of what makes poetry *poetry*, distinguishing it from other forms of writing. In poetic writings, there's mostly *show* and very little *tell*. Imagery is represented in poetry by appealing to our five senses and by the use of symbolic language. For example, in this excerpt from a poem called "Run Ablaze," the imagery of someone in cardiac distress being attended by God is powerful:

> *Take hold of my chest*
> *Firmly place your word*
> *Begin compressions*
> *Keep blood*
> *Circulating within me*
> *Defibrillate this heart*
> *May it only be synced*
> *To the rhythm of your word*
> *Intubate my soul*
> *May my mind never forget*[7]

We know, almost automatically, that the poem contains symbolic and figurative language we are not meant to take literally. God is not actually taking hold of someone's physical chest and placing His Word inside it. No one is truly getting intubated. The language is figurative, symbolic, imaginative, evoking word pictures and emotion and connection. When we read poetry, we read not as observers but as participants.

Someone recently gifted our family a virtual reality headset, and my kids were really excited about it. I didn't understand what all the hype was about and thought, "How lame (I'm sure my use of the word *lame* is lame)! It's like a Wii or like playing a video game with a headset on, right?" In my mind I compared it to the old-school View-Master, which let you insert slides in the top of a viewer and click through to see different pictures. A few months later, for a date night, my husband and I went to an immersive digital art space, where we felt as if we had been transported inside a virtual reality game. It was an amazing experience of sensory overload! Needless to say, as soon as we got home, I decided to try my children's virtual reality device. Just as in the digital art space, I felt transported, like a participant in another world. I could pick up virtual items, recreate virtual rooms, and play virtual games.

Immersive is how we should read biblical poetry. We not only recite the poems and sing the songs and pray the prayers along with the poet, but we allow our imaginations to draw us into the experience that the images evoke so we might feel and see and respond in the way that the poem is calling us to.

TRANSFORM YOUR
STUDY OF POETRY

Parallelism, strophes, and stanzas are used literarily in Hebrew poetry to clarify the imagery being used in the poem, simplify a complex idea, enter the full emotional experience expressed by the poem, and provide a model for praying and singing and worshiping God. It is through the poetic genre that we encounter a full range of human emotion, where we see that it's okay to "keep it real" with God, and where we learn that all of ourselves can be offered in worship to God.

To transform your study of poetry, pay attention to the parallelism, strophes, and stanzas that indicate correlations or shifts in topic, theme, or imagery. If there are inscriptions that indicate the occasion for a psalm, you can read the corresponding event that it refers to for historical context. You may also want to consider how the poem fits with similar psalms (psalms of thanksgiving, lament, etc.) or check to see if that psalm is quoted in the New Testament. I find it helpful to print out a copy of the passage without the paragraph markings so I can do my own work and not rely on the help given in my study Bible.

Use Psalm 3 to work through some of the principles from this chapter.

1. Read the psalm at least three times in one sitting, as it is very short.

2. On your third read, make note of the parallelism. How do the parallel lines correspond? In other words, what is being repeated, contrasted, explained, or expanded upon?

3. Make note of any imagery throughout the psalm.

4. Engage your senses and emotions in the reading of the psalm. How is the poem directing you to feel? What is it that you see through David's eyes?

5. What do you learn about God in this psalm?

6. What do you learn about humanity (David, his enemies)?

7. Do we experience situations comparable to David's? If so, how? If not, why not?

8. Given David's response to his situation, what should our response be to ours?

9. How might we read verse 7 literally? How might we read verse 7 *literarily*?

10. Should we ask God to "break the teeth" of our enemies? Why or why not?

6

A WORD FROM THE WISE
(Wisdom)

Let the wise hear and increase in learning,
and the one who understands obtain guidance,
to understand a proverb and a saying,
the words of the wise and their riddles.

PROVERBS 1:5-6

My grandma Nicie (pronounced NIE-see) used to say, "If you watch your friends, then your foes can't hurt you." I heard her say it many times as I was growing up and don't remember much about what situations called this saying to mind for her. However, whenever she would say it, I'd roll it over in my mind for days, trying to understand what it meant. Now I think I do. She's equating friends to foes, saying that those people whom you consider friends may actually be enemies; so you basically can't trust your friends because in the end, they may turn out to be your foe. This seemed like such a pessimistic view of friendship! I thought, *Maybe you should get better friends, Grandma!* Then I watched a video of an old evangelist plucking on his guitar and belting out the words that echoed my grandma's familiar quote: "Your close friend, your close friend / Your enemy cannot harm you, but watch your close friend."[1] Then I understood that Grandma Nicie and the old evangelist were referencing the account of Judas betraying Jesus from Matthew 26:47–50. It says:

> *While he was still speaking, Judas came, one of the twelve, and with him a great crowd with swords and clubs, from the chief priests and the elders of the people. Now the betrayer had given them a sign, saying, "The one I will kiss is the man; seize him." And he came up to Jesus at once and said, "Greetings, Rabbi!" And he kissed him. Jesus said to him, "Friend, do what you came to do." Then they came up and laid hands on Jesus and seized him.*

It was starting to make some sense—but I kept pondering it. Is the application of this passage a warning to watch our friends, especially those close to you because they might someday betray you? If so, I would have to edit my friend list drastically! But I don't think that is the intent of this passage. While it highlights Judas's hypocrisy in calling himself a follower of Christ, kissing Him as his friend, and then betraying Jesus by turning Him over to the authorities, the main application of this passage has less to do with human relationships and more to do with our relationship with Christ. What are ways that hypocrisy shows up in our lives, between what we profess and what we do? I see how my grandma and the songwriter got it twisted. It's a common problem that many of us have as we approach the Bible. We make ourselves the hero or the victim and everyone else the bad guy. In reality, as we study the Scriptures and try to make applications to our lives today, we should see ourselves not as the Christ figure in the story, nor the hero, nor the noble king. Instead, we should see ourselves as the ordinary Israelite, the bystander in the crowd, or a person who is responding to Jesus. This will greatly help us as we study any book of the Bible, but also as we think about wisdom literature.

WHAT IS WISDOM LITERATURE?

Wisdom literature includes the books of Job, Proverbs, Ecclesiastes, and Song of Solomon, which primarily contain verses and sayings that provide wisdom for living daily under God's rule and care. Remember that the entire Bible is God's inspired, authoritative Word for His people. All that exists comes from Him, including all wisdom. Proverbs points to this: "The LORD by wisdom founded the earth; by understanding he established the heavens; by his knowledge the deeps broke open, and the clouds drop down the dew" (3:19–20), and so does another wisdom book, Job: "With God are wisdom and might; he has counsel and understanding" (12:13). Out of God's love and concern for all His creation, He gave us wisdom to guide our lives in godliness, to build our character, and to strengthen our faith in Him. Though wisdom is a gift, we are encouraged to seek the wisdom of God:

> *Yes, if you call out for insight*
> *and raise your voice for understanding,*
> *if you seek it like silver*
> *and search for it as for hidden treasures,*
> *then you will understand the fear of the LORD*
> *and find the knowledge of God.*

For the LORD *gives wisdom;*
  from his mouth come knowledge and understanding;
  he stores up sound wisdom for the upright;
    he is a shield to those who walk in integrity,
guarding the paths of justice
    and watching over the way of his saints.
Then you will understand righteousness and justice
    and equity, every good path;
  for wisdom will come into your heart,
    and knowledge will be pleasant to your soul;
discretion will watch over you,
    understanding will guard you. (Proverbs 2:3–11)

In ancient biblical culture, wise men were common. Pharaoh consulted Egyptian wise men when they attempted to re-create God's plagues on Egypt (Exodus 7:11). King Xerxes consulted wise men before responding to Queen Vashti's refusal to parade herself before his drunken entourage (Esther 1:13). Job's friends were considered wise men (Job 34:2). Many kings and emperors employed wise men to provide insight for their rulers on important matters. But of all the wise men who ever lived or ever will live, none were wiser than King Solomon (1 Kings 3:12). His humble prayer to God, asking for discernment to govern well as king, was answered abundantly by God with not only wisdom but riches and honor that would follow him as long as he fully committed himself to God and obeyed His commandments (1 Kings 3:13–14). With that wisdom, Solomon's fame grew. Solomon wrote more than three thousand proverbs and a thousand songs. He was versed in botany, horticulture, marine biology, animal science, and more. Included among the proverbs and songs of Solomon are the books of Proverbs, Ecclesiastes, and Song of Solomon.

The primary feature of wisdom literature is proverbs. Proverbs are short, memorable statements of truth, presented through the poetic form of parallelism, and often replete with metaphors and similes. We discussed parallelism in chapter 5, where a set of lines are related to each other in some way. The second and subsequent lines repeat (synonymous), contrast (antithetical), compare (emblematic), complete (synthetic), or extend the thought (staircase) of the first line. A metaphor compares two unrelated things by calling it something that it is not but relating the two in a meaningful way. For example, "Your eyes are doves behind your veil" (Song of Solomon 4:1). A simile compares two unrelated things using the words *like* or *as* in the comparison. For example, "Your hair is like a flock of goats leaping down the slopes of Gilead" (Song of Solomon 4:1). Part of the difficulty in studying wisdom literature is its unrelenting, creative use of symbolic language. Sometimes it's difficult to identify what all the figurative language is referencing and then how to apply it to a contemporary context. If we don't have the context of what the slopes of Gilead were like and if we can't visualize a flock of goats leaping down them, that simile will not make much sense to our modern ears. It doesn't sound like the most flattering statement. It reminds me of an old, popular situation comedy that featured two teenagers head over heels for each other. The young man would often try to impress his girlfriend by complimenting her using highly figurative and, in his mind, romantic terms. When he tested out a new flattering metaphor to describe his girlfriend or their love, she would gush over his words, while the rest of their friends and family stared in bewilderment, not understanding what the metaphor really meant. This is not how it's supposed to work with wisdom literature;

it wasn't meant to be confusing. All of Scripture was meant to be understood, believed, and appropriately applied in light of Christ's redemptive work.

UNDERSTANDING WISDOM LITERARILY

Particularly in wisdom literature, the literary and cultural contexts provide helpful clues to understanding a passage. It will always be a help to any student of the Bible to read the passages surrounding our main text to aid our understanding. We want to enter the world of the original audience and see with their eyes, from their perspective, so we don't inadvertently impose meaning that is not there or miss meaning we should take from the passage. Just as narratives and poetry help us enter into real-life experiences and emotions, so does wisdom literature. The greatest benefit that context brings to our study of wisdom literature is that *Aha!* factor that helps us see even more clearly the point of a passage.

JOB

The book of Job is tough! This righteous man has everything taken from him by Satan, with the approval of God, and Job has no idea why calamity has hit him so hard. The entire book is devoted to Job's friends wrestling to convince Job that he somehow deserved what he was suffering. Literarily, the book opens and closes with narrative bookends. The opening narrative sets the context for the remainder of the book, and it concludes with God shutting the friends down for not speaking of God what was right (Job 42:7–8), and with God abundantly restoring Job's fortunes and family.

The main theme of this book seems to be the sovereignty of God in suffering. As you study Job, keep this theme in mind. The difficulty in Job is making sense of the friends' counsel. While we can accept much of their advice as generally true, which is the case for all proverbial wisdom, very little of their advice is true or applicable in Job's specific situation. The mystery is why we need to spend so much space in the pages of Scripture on advice and counsel that Job can't even use. Remember that wisdom literature draws us into the realities of everyday situations and struggles. We can all relate to having circumstances in our lives that our friends attempt to help us walk through, but their "help" is anything but helpful. We can learn from poor examples as much as we can learn from the positive ones. The intentions of Job's counselors were commendable (Job 2:11–13) even though their advice was generally off. We see in Job's responses to each of his friends' speeches that Job understands that their advice is flawed. We can sense his frustration, and at one point he says,

> *I have heard many things like these.*
> *You are all miserable comforters.*
> *Is there no end to your empty words?*
> *What provokes you that you continue testifying?*
> *If you were in my place I could also talk like you.*
> *I could string words together against you*
> *and shake my head at you.*
> *Instead, I would encourage you with my mouth,*
> *and the consolation from my lips would bring relief.*
> *(Job 16:1–5 CSB)*

Job is literally over it! So when we read the counsel of his friends, we can, as the adage goes, "eat the meat and toss the bones." In other words, take what is good and right and helpful generally. In other contexts, their counsel might be right on point. Job even owns up to his own rash words (6:3) and, near the end of his battle, repents for his ignorance and rash speech (42:1–6). When studying the friends' counsel, read their advice in conjunction with Job's response. Isolate stanzas and strophes to pick up topics Job's friends address. Note any virtues and vices, proverbial wisdom, statements that don't apply to Job, and how their responses inform how we might counsel a friend who is suffering today.

PROVERBS

While Proverbs often seem to offer basic life lessons for anyone, whether they are Christian or not, they are rooted in the wisdom of God and meant for us to use them to walk by faith in the power of His grace. God who dispenses His wisdom according to His divine purposes will protect us, guard our paths, and give us understanding and discretion. The problem of interpretation goes beyond my grandma's quote or a bluesy gospel song. Interpretation is a common problem in approaching the wisdom literature of the Bible, and especially the book of Proverbs. The Proverbs are not rules to obey or promises from God, but everyday wisdom that serves as a guide for wise living in a wicked world. The classic example for this idea is Proverbs 22:6, which says, "Train up a child in the way he should go; even when he is old he will not depart from it." This is not a guarantee that good parenting results in children who don't stray. We see the implied command to train up our children in the way they should go, but we leave the results to God, understanding that this proverb holds generally, but when sinful hearts are involved, of both parents and children, there are no guarantees.

Proverbs is set in the context of a father giving wise instructions to his son. His tone is pastoral and tender but also straightforward. The overall themes in this book are shaped by its main divisions. Chapters 1–9 fit together as a unit. Wisdom and Folly are personified as women. The section focuses on the contrast between Ms. Wisdom and Ms. Folly, calling the son to choose the way of wisdom. From there, chapters 10–20 are a somewhat-disorderly collection of proverbs by Solomon, but they are marked by mostly antithetical parallelism, where one line gives an instruction, way to live, or attitude of heart and mind, while the other line presents what the contrast would be, often using the word *but* to indicate the shift. The positive aspect of the parallelism may be the first or second line. There doesn't seem to be a clear pattern one way or the other. For example, Proverbs 10:23 says, "Doing wrong is like a joke to a fool, but wisdom is pleasure to a man of understanding." We see the contrasting idea that while a fool takes pleasure in wrongdoing, people of understanding take pleasure in wisdom. There are also plenty of examples of synonymous parallelism, where the same idea is communicated in slightly different wording, such as "From the fruit of a man's mouth his stomach is satisfied; he is satisfied by the yield of his lips" (Proverbs 18:20). Here, the same idea and similar wording is used in both lines. As you read and meditate on the Proverbs, pay attention to the various types of parallelism and allow it to inform the meaning you gain from the text.

ECCLESIASTES

Ecclesiastes opens (1:1–11) and closes (12:9–13) in the third-person point of view, where a narrator is providing commentary on the main character in the book, known as "the Preacher," who is probably Solomon or one of his descendants. These opening and closing verses serve as bookends that introduce the main theme and tone of the book—namely, that all is vanity, mist, fleeting, meaningless. So the tone is a bit depressing. Ecclesiastes 1:3 poses the main question that the entire book addresses. It says, "What does man gain by all the toil at which he toils under the sun?" The closing verses answer this burning question. In between, throughout the rest of the book, the content hammers the idea that *everything* is meaningless—wisdom, pleasure, one's life legacy, work, wealth, honor. It's all meaningless. What then, does give meaning to life? The Preacher hints at it when he talks about enjoying life as a gift from God (2:24–26), honoring God in word and deed (5:1–6), fearing God (8:12). Amid all the evil and emptiness of this life, what brings fullness is fearing and obeying God. The narrator concludes with these words, "The end of the matter; all has been heard. Fear God and keep his commandments, for this is the whole duty of man" (Ecclesiastes 12:13).

SONG OF SOLOMON

Song of Solomon makes some Christians blush for its romantic overtones and highly sensual imagery. It's an intimate love story that follows a young couple from their "You had me at hello" moment through their courtship and marriage. While we may not connect completely with some of the metaphors they use to express the depth of their love and admiration of each other, we get the picture. They are head over heels in love, and everyone knows it. Their friends even cheer them on (Song of Solomon 1:4).

Some place this book within the poetic genre. Others place it within wisdom literature. While the entirety of the book is poetic, I chose to place it in the wisdom genre because it parallels the other wisdom literature in allowing us to see and experience life vicariously through this couple. In Song of Solomon we see true, romantic love awakened in its appropriate time. This is a wise word for our modern age that glamorizes promiscuity and encourages high levels of intimacy and low levels of commitment in romantic relationships. To be satisfied with one's true love is a basic human longing that the Song of Solomon dramatizes with brilliance.

A difficulty with studying the Song of Solomon is understanding it in light of God's redemptive purposes. One solution is to spiritualize the book, suggesting that the groom symbolizes Christ, the bride symbolizes the church, and that this whole book is an allegory about Christ and the church. While I can agree that the Song of Solomon is likely not an account of one specific, real couple and can respect the alternate view, I think this book can be read more naturally as symbolizing and illuminating romantic love. It seems to be a stretch to make it about Christ. We do know that all of Scripture is about Jesus, but it's not about Jesus in the same way. As intimate and romantic and committed as these two lovers are, the Scriptures teach us that there is a love that is deeper, more intimate, and greater than earthly love. It is the love of Christ for His bride the church. When Christ returns for His bride, there will be another wedding and banquet and celebration of holy love for all eternity. We don't have to over-spiritualize Song of Solomon to see this connection. These match-made-in-heaven lovers want their beloved to know that they are seen and cherished for who they are, exactly how God has made them to be. They are observant and specific. They know the value of waiting and how waiting produces longing and how longing will be satisfied in due time. As Christians, we know this too, not only in regard to romantic love but in our longing to see our Savior and in seeing Him to be satisfied (Psalm 107:9).

TRANSFORM YOUR STUDY OF WISDOM LITERATURE

When studying the wisdom books, keep in mind the overall themes of each book and study a single passage in light of that theme. The writer of each book seems to be on a journey looking for specific aspects of wisdom. Job wants an answer to the problem of suffering. The writer of Proverbs wants to know how to live wisely and not foolishly. The "preacher" in Ecclesiastes (1:1) is looking for meaning in a life filled with empty vanities. The lovers in Song of Solomon want to keep their love alive. The images and metaphors and proverbs in each book are meant to expand your understanding, so when reading them, keep it simple.

1. Read Song of Solomon 4:1 and determine what type of parallelism you think it is.

2. Note any metaphors or similes.

3. What is the main point that is being communicated?

4. Read all of Song of Solomon chapter 4.

5. What emotions does this passage invoke?

6. What does this passage teach you about romantic relationships or marriage?

7. In a few words, what is the groom celebrating in his bride?

8. What does Christ celebrate in His bride, the church?

7

VISIONS OF THE FUTURE
(Prophecy)

No one loves the messenger who brings bad news.

SOPHOCLES, ANTIGONE

Have you ever had to be the bearer of bad news? It's no fun, and it's even worse to have to constantly deliver bad news daily. This sometimes happens to healthcare workers who are caring for a patient whose health is in decline. They carry the burden of having to provide dire news to people who are holding out hope for just a sliver of good news—and having to watch the faces of those loved ones whose hopes are dashed with each successive report. When my own sister was in the hospital for several weeks, we began thinking her condition would require a relatively simple procedure, but her situation turned out to be complicated and dangerous. She needed surgery and every option presented significant risks, including a surgery with only a 30-percent survival rate. As a family, we prayed and listened to healthcare professionals who were obligated to report to us options that ranged from bad to worst. My sister survived that surgery, and we remember with thankfulness the Lord's mercy, as well as the courage of those care providers whose job it was to prepare us for the worst.

We often think of Old Testament prophets as the bearers of bad news. They continually stood before God's people detailing their idolatrous and wicked behavior and warning of God's judgment. Would the slivers of hope that peeked through their message be enough for the prophet to hold on to, trusting that Israel would repent and turn back to God? I'm sure they wondered why God would entrust His Word to them to share with such a wayward people. Theologian Gary V. Smith suggests, "God did not give his people his words to make them smart; he spoke so that they would respond with love, fear, service, obedience, and worship."[1] The prophet's job was difficult, but their calling built their faith to believe that God's people would indeed hear the message and turn back to Him in loving obedience and worship.

WHAT IS PROPHECY?

Prophecy is the inspired communication of God's Word through a human agent. Prophets were God's spokespersons, whom He called to communicate specific messages to His people. Those prophetic messages included proclamation of God's love for and faithfulness toward His people, details of their rebellion, an opportunity for repentance with accompanying blessings, and warning of judgment if they continued in sin. When considering the prophetic books as a genre, we often divide them into two categories: the major prophets and the minor prophets. Major prophets are those that make up the larger prophetic books that cover large spans of Israel's history—Isaiah, Jeremiah, Lamentations, Ezekiel, and Daniel. Minor prophets are the smaller books with a narrower focus—Hosea, Joel, Amos, Obadiah, Jonah, Micah, Nahum, Habakkuk, Zephaniah, Haggai, Zechariah, and Malachi. We name them according to the prophet who wrote that particular book, except for Lamentations, with the author unnamed but widely considered to be the prophet Jeremiah.

God used prophets to speak the cold, hard truth to His cold, hard people. When reading the prophets, have the book of Deuteronomy bookmarked. Deuteronomy details God's instructions to Israel, retelling their wilderness journeys of more than forty years, reiterating the law for the new generation of Israelites on the cusp of entering the Promised Land with Joshua, and encouraging the Israelites' faithfulness toward God for their good and for their witness to the surrounding nations. No sooner had they entered the Promised Land than they began "wilding out," practicing the idolatry of foreign lands, marrying outside the covenant community, doing all the things the Lord had warned them against and commanded them not to do (Deuteronomy 7:1–4).

Prophecy is hard because reading it always feels like you're jumping into the middle of a story. The context of the oracles (speeches or announcements from God to the people) are sometimes hard to discern. If you're unfamiliar with the history of Israel, here it is in a nutshell. God very specifically gave them instruction about how they were to live as His people in the Promised Land. He warned them against going after the gods of those lands into idolatry. He promised blessing upon them for living in loving, faithful obedience

and promised judgment and destruction upon them for disobedience. The people did exactly the opposite of what God
had instructed, and God—who is faithful and fulfills all His
promises—did exactly what He said He would do if they
failed to obey Him, namely giving them over to a foreign
nation as captives where they would serve foreign gods (Deuteronomy 28:36). However, their captives would "not respect
the old or show mercy to the young" (Deuteronomy 28:50).
These captives would decimate the people, bringing them to
the brink of ruin and destruction (Deuteronomy 28:63). The
Israelites would become a scattered people.

Israel and Judah were warring sibling nations that had once
been one nation under the great King David, the man after
God's own heart. Sibling rivalry got the best of them after
the death of King David, who had promised the kingship
to Solomon even though he was not next in line as the el-
dest of David's sons. Adonijah had set himself up as the next
king (1 Kings 1:5), though he knew David had promised the
kingship to Solomon. Actually it was God who had chosen
Solomon to succeed David (1 Chronicles 28:1–7). Solomon's
mom, Bathsheba, and the priest Nathan thwarted Adonijah's
attempted coup (1 Kings 1:11–27). King Solomon took the
reins after David's death, rebuilt the temple, re-established
worship in the temple, became filthy rich and super-wise.
Then he too started "wilding," marrying women from pagan
nations and worshiping and building temples for their gods,
in effect turning his heart from fully following and trusting
the Lord. How could the wisest man on the planet turn to
such foolishness?! Though wise, Solomon's heart was decep-
tive (Jeremiah 17:9). The Lord took the kingdom from Solomon's son Rehoboam, and left him with one tribe out of the

twelve tribes of Israel (1 Kings 11:11–13, 36). Ten of those tribes went to Jeroboam, Solomon's servant and a bit of an opportunist (1 Kings 11:26–31). Rehoboam would be left only with the tribe of Judah (1 Kings 12:17–20).

This splitting of the kingdom is one of the most pivotal points in Israel's history, since it was the beginning of the divided kingdoms of Israel in the north, with Samaria as its capital city, and Judah in the south, with Jerusalem as its capital city. From that point on, a slew of kings ruled each kingdom, mostly leading the people further into idolatry and further away from the Lord. Not only that, but each kingdom was constantly barraged by invaders who capitalized on their vulnerabilities. Out of the twenty-one kings of Judah, only five honored God and sought to govern according to His word as it was handed down from Moses. Of the kings of Israel, there were nineteen, and none of them ruled righteously nor gave up their idolatrous ways, nor encouraged the people to do so. In fact, it was the exact opposite. These kings continued to lead the people in worshiping and building altars to idols.

The failure of the myriad of kings who ruled the divided kingdoms of Israel and Judah leaves us yearning for just one righteous king. Surely they needed a king who would honor God and teach the people His ways, one who would build God's kingdom, a kingdom that would never end and that the gates of hell would not prevail against. Here's yet another Easter egg—a hint pointing to a future king and His kingdom. Thousands of years later, a king would come on the scene who would be born in humble circumstances, who would not take power by force or military might or conniving, but with humility and grace and self-sacrifice. This king would not only teach people the Word of God and the ways of God, but He would perfectly obey the law of God. He would not only occupy the office of King, but also that of Priest and Prophet. Indeed, this king is none other than the King of glory, Jesus Christ the righteous. Jesus Christ the mediator. Jesus Christ, the great prophet who speaks the word of God to the people because He is God in the flesh.

To grasp the great burden of the prophets, you must understand this sad history of God's people. Take some time to read all of Deuteronomy as well as 1 and 2 Kings over the next few weeks, as these passages provide such vital historical context for understanding the prophets. I realize that many people hate history, perhaps because learning it in a school context didn't always make it real or fresh. History is hard, with so many people, dates, and details to remember. But the story of God's people is a part of your story and will serve you in all your days of reading God's Word.

Prophecy is also hard because often the prophets are warning of events that are yet to happen. Those events can be immediate (as in the prophet's lifetime) or intermediate (as in the time of Christ), or eschatological (EH-ska-tuh-LAH-juh-kuhl, as in the end of time).[2] The prophets are trying to convince stony-hearted people that they are deeply enmeshed in their sin and that the Lord will judge them for it if they don't repent, but that the Lord will faithfully forgive and restore them if they do turn away from their sin.

UNDERSTANDING PROPHECY LITERARILY

As literature, prophecy is sort of like short State of the Union addresses. These messages emphasize pressing issues facing the nation of Israel (their sin) and provide God's solution to their problems (repentance). Sometimes it seems as if the prophets repeat themselves a lot. This may be because several prophets are contemporaries and are prophesying during the same time period. For example, Jeremiah prophesied across fifty years, so his ministry coincided with prophets like Zephaniah, Habakkuk, Ezekiel, and Daniel. You will read echoes of similar messages among these prophets. Also, prophets like Jeremiah or Hosea had ministries that spanned many years, so their speeches were given months or even years apart. Even a short book like Hosea could contain dozens of messages that he gave over a long time and through reigns of several different kings. It's hard for us to grasp this, but just think how weird it would be to read, one after another, dozens of posts from the same blogger who was writing the posts from 2010 until today. There's bound to be a bit of repetition. God often communicates these messages to the prophets as poetry or oracles.

Poetry

The prophets use mostly poetry and what is called *poetic prose* to communicate God's message to the people. Why poetry? Think about it. If the State of the Union address for the United States was delivered as a rap, many of us might repeat and recite it, whether or not we liked the message. How many times have we recited a familiar tune, even though we didn't really care for the song at all? The nature of poetry begs for memorization and recitation. Second, with poetry, the prophets can pack in lots of information with fewer words. Poetry offers an economy of words that opens up a world of imagination. Poetry lends itself to memorization, recitation, and drama with the use of images that stir the imagination and help the people see in vivid figurative language how God sees their situations and what He plans to do about it. A leading voice on prophetic literature writes, "Poetry appeals more directly to the whole person than prose does. It stimulates our imaginations, arouses our emotions, feeds our intellects, and addresses our wills. Perhaps this is why poetry is the preferred mode of communication of the prophets, whose purpose depends on capturing the attention of their listeners and persuading them their message is urgent."[3]

The conveyed emotion of prophecy is God's anger over sin, the prophets' grief, and the people's revelry and ignorance of their plight. The tone is one of warning and judgment. In most of the prophets, we see God's perspective and the perspective of the prophet, but we do not often hear from the people themselves. We just get the report of their continuing in sin or of their repentance. For example, Isaiah writes about people not listening to the message: "The people did not turn to him who struck them, nor inquire of the LORD of hosts" (Isaiah 9:13). Jonah narrates a time when the people did respond to God: "When God saw what they did, how they turned from their evil way, God relented of the disaster that he had said he would do to them, and he did not do it" (Jonah 3:10).

There is some narrative in almost all of the prophets, but the vast majority of prophetic writing is poetry. When we read books like the Psalms, the parallelism and symmetry of lines are key to our understanding. Within the prophecy genre, parallelism is there, but the vividness of the lines comes through additional literary devices such as metaphor, personification, and apostrophe. A metaphor compares two things that are not literally related. A very familiar example would be Isaiah 64:8: "But now, O LORD, you are our Father; we are the clay, and you are our potter; we are all the work of your hand." In this example, God is compared to a potter and the people of God compared to clay. God is not a literal potter, and people are not clay, but this comparison provides a view of God as a master designer who controls and shapes every aspect of human existence. Personification gives human characteristics to nonhuman things. We read in Ezekiel 27:28: "At the sound of the cry of your pilots the countryside shakes" (pilots are sailors). The countryside shakes—shivering, which is a human activity. When seas shout or mountains cry, these are examples of personification because the seas and mountains are doing things people do. An apostrophe speaks to an inanimate thing as if it were human. In Isaiah 49:13 the Lord commands the heavens and earth and mountains to sing: "Sing for joy, O heavens, and exult, O earth; break forth, O mountains, into singing!" It's helpful to understand these categories when reading the Bible because they are clear clues for us not to read the passage literally, as if mountains were really singing. Instead, we are to use our imaginations and emotions to enter into the scene as a participant so we can see the emphasis of the passage.

Oracles

An oracle is a pronouncement from God given through His spokesperson, often in a vision or dream.[4] The books of prophecy are full of oracles. The main thrust of the prophets is "thus says the Lord." It is true that "what we read in the Prophetic Books, then, is not merely God's word as the prophet saw it but God's word as God wished the prophet to present it. The prophet does not act or speak independently of God."[5] In most of the oracles, God is making His purpose and expectation and plans very clear so the people have no excuse. He announces, explains, and provides reasons and consequences. He also holds out glimmers of hope so people would not just be fearful of judgment but so they would also desire God's blessing and deliverance.

In many oracles, God urges His people to turn away from sin and return to relationship with Him. Some of these "judgment oracles" contain judgment or the threat of judgment (Zephaniah 2:4). Even while the judgment oracles warn of punishment, their purpose is to encourage individuals or nations to repent. In some oracles, God calls for repentance, provides His reasons, and then urges people to confess and turn away from their sin. Another type of judgment oracle is the woe oracle. A "woe" is a cry of lament or distress, often in combination with weeping, sackcloth, ashes, and tearing of the clothes. In a woe oracle, there's the pronouncement of woe against a people or nation, the reason for the pronouncement, and then cries of lament and judgment, all with the goal of seeing true repentance, obedience, and love toward God (Habakkuk 2:6–19).

A second broad category of oracles is courtroom-type oracles. These oracles include God as judge, jury, and executioner of any sentencing. They open with a summons, followed by God's charges against His audience and the threat of judgment to be rendered as a result of guilt before God. Among the courtroom oracles are lawsuit, trial, and dispute oracles. Think of a lawsuit oracle like our courtrooms today with a plaintiff, defendant, witnesses, charges, and sentencing. The trial oracle actually walks through the evidence logically and renders a verdict. God is portrayed as judge, jury, and executioner of the sentence associated with the charges (Hosea 4–10). Sometimes an oracle deals with disputes between individuals and would be handled among the leaders of a community.

Finally, there are deliverance oracles. These point to God's deliverance of His people from their sins and from their enemies. Salvation oracles rehearse God's plan of deliverance for His people. They are marked by an opening address to His audience, recounting what He has done in the past and remembering God's promise to save or to avenge so that His people would have hope and trust in His promise to be with them and deliver them (Obadiah 17–21). Future-salvation oracles focus primarily on God's future acts of salvation in the end times. They also review God's past acts of salvation and often include a response from the people.

In addition to these oracles, there are also hymns and visions scattered throughout the prophetic literature.[6] The point of mentioning all the oracles and what to look for in them is so we might come to the prophetic books with more confidence, enter into the dramatic force of them, and work to see the beauty of Christ in the midst of so much darkness.

TRANSFORM YOUR STUDY OF PROPHECY

Prophecy shows that the metanarrative of Scripture is still moving forward. It demonstrates the seamlessness of Scripture in God calling a people out for Himself (Genesis), handing down His laws (re-articulated in Deuteronomy), in the people failing to obey (see 2 Kings 25), in God using the prophets to urge the people to repent and providing them with post-judgment hope. As you read and study the prophets, take note of how Christ is the greater fulfillment of the prophets' messages.

Answer the following questions using what you have learned from this chapter.

1. What type of oracle is Amos 4:1–5?

2. What type of oracle is Habakkuk 2:6–14?

3. What type of oracle is Isaiah 40:1–5?

4. Use Lamentations 3[7] to find:

   • the type(s) of oracle(s) in this chapter.
   • examples of metaphor and personification.
   • how the parallelism in each strophe intensifies the imagery.
   • God's primary message to His people.
   • how this passage compares or contrasts with the life and message of Jesus.
   • what this passage prompts you to believe or change.

8

THE GOOD NEWS
(Gospels)

Some say that writing a biography is pursuing a "fleeting figure"
from the past "in such way as to bring them alive in the present."
BIOGRAPHER RICHARD HOLMES

Muhammad Ali was a gold-medal Olympian, three-
time heavyweight boxing champion, a humanitarian
and activist. He won numerous awards that deemed him
"the greatest of all time," including the Presidential Medal of
Freedom in 2005.[1] He was unmatched by his own admission,
and his "I am the greatest" speech is truly unforgettable—
and hilarious. He once bragged that he was too great to be
humble.[2] He didn't wait for greatness to be conferred upon
him; he asserted it himself. But does greatness come through
self-assertion, goodwill, accomplishments, and pride? Surely
not. I would not doubt that much of Muhammad Ali's bra-
vado was a bit of "trash talk" to intimidate the competition,
and it seemed to work! His pre- and post-fight interviews

were almost as legendary as his wins against boxing greats like Sonny Liston, Joe Frazier, and George Foreman.

The Scriptures give us a totally different picture of greatness. Jesus said that the greatest is the one who is servant of all (Matthew 20:26). He came "not to be served but to serve, and to give his life as a ransom for many" (Matthew 20:28). Though He is God, Jesus did not boast about His greatness but came as a humble servant to proclaim the kingdom of God. How does one capture this kind of greatness? How would the Gospel writers demonstrate Christ's greatness, His power, and His authority, and how would they convince people of who Jesus was without prideful boasting? The accounts in the Gospels of Jesus' life are not just biographical or even mostly biographical. They are theological, and they have eternal impact for us as soon as His words hit our eyes and ears and hearts.

WHAT ARE THE GOSPELS?

The Gospels are the New Testament books of Matthew, Mark, Luke, and John. They are primarily narrative, but we treat them separately from Old Testament narratives because the Gospels center on the gospel of Jesus Christ as it was proclaimed during His earthly ministry. *Gospel* means good news, so the good news of Christ's life, ministry, death, resurrection, and return dominates every book. The book of Mark, which was most likely the first of the Gospels written, about thirty years after Christ's resurrection, even opens with these words: "The beginning of the gospel of Jesus Christ, the Son of God" (Mark 1:1). The Gospels chronicle Jesus' life and ministry up to His death and resurrection. Luke wrote the book of Acts, and it centers on the work of the Holy Spirit in carrying forward the gospel throughout the establishment and growth of the church. We include Acts here in the same genre category with the Gospels because Luke and Acts are companion books, with Acts as a continuation of Luke's Gospel. Together, the Gospels and Acts read like an anthology, or a collection, that contains lots of other subgenres like hero stories, miracle stories, parables, eyewitness accounts, and of course the passion story that details the final week of Jesus' earthly ministry culminating in His crucifixion, death, and resurrection. Besides stories, the Gospels and Acts contain elements of almost every other genre, from speeches to poetry to wisdom literature to prophetic to apocalyptic literature.

The words of Jesus are prominent in the Gospels as well. He preached and taught small groups of disciples to large crowds. He taught in the temple and on the streets and in homes. His primary message was "proclaiming the gospel of God, and saying, 'The time is fulfilled, and the kingdom of God is at hand; repent and believe in the gospel'" (Mark 1:14–15). Jesus intentionally used figures of speech in His sermons and teaching (John 16:25), typified by the use of metaphors (such as, "You are the salt of the earth," in Matthew 5:13), exaggerated speech ("If anyone comes to me and does not hate his own father and mother and wife and children and brothers and sisters, yes, and even his own life, he cannot be my disciple" in Luke 14:26), and parables (such as the parable of the sower in Matthew 13:3–23).

Synoptic Gospels

Within the Gospels, Matthew, Mark, and Luke are referred to as "synoptic" because their content and structures are very similar. They open with an introduction and include John the Baptist's ministry, Jesus' baptism and temptation, Jesus' ministry throughout Galilee and into Samaria and Judea, passion week, Jesus' death, and His resurrection. All three books give great attention to Jesus' teachings on the kingdom of God. Not only does much of the shared material follow the same ordering of events, they also share the same wording. This may be because Mark's Gospel is commonly believed to have been written first and that Matthew and Luke used Mark's work as a sort of template.

The book of John doesn't follow the same pattern as the synoptic Gospels. Much of the information in John's Gospel is new material not included in the other Gospels. The synoptics center around Jesus' ministry in Galilee while John focuses more on Jesus' ministry in Jerusalem. The synoptics start with the genealogy and birth of Jesus, where John starts with creation and establishes Jesus as the Word who became flesh and dwelt among us, from whom we have received grace and truth (John 1:14, 16–17).

Though Mark is generally regarded as the first of the Gospel writers, there is still some disagreement about which book came first, who copied whom, and how and if one should merge the details of each parallel story into one complete unit. For example, some would try to combine all the details of the passion narrative from each of the Gospels to get a more complete picture of Jesus' final days on earth. While this might be greatly helpful in some ways, merging the stories runs the risk of missing the intent of each Gospel author as they highlighted specific details. Each Gospel writer presented details, quotes, and emphases in the way he wanted the narrative to be received. The Gospel writers made decisions to include or exclude certain details based on their unique writing perspective, their purposes for writing, and the specific audiences they were trying to address. While filling in details from a parallel Gospel may be helpful, we should also aim to take each writer's version on its own terms and see how it fits into the overall message of the book, and how it uniquely contributes to the overall message of the Bible.

Acts

The book of Acts also does not follow the same structure as the Gospels. It is a continuation of the book of Luke and resembles a personal letter, especially at the beginning (Acts 1:1), when Luke addresses the work to the same Theophilus mentioned in Luke 1:3. Acts is primarily focused on the activity of the Holy Spirit in the growth of the early church, from Jerusalem to Judea to Samaria to the end of the earth (Luke 24:46–49; Acts 1:1–8, 2:1–21). It resembles an epic adventure story, with heroes such as Peter and Paul establishing the church and spreading the gospel of Jesus Christ from coast to coast with the help of the unseen hero who permeates the book, the Holy Spirit. As you study Acts, notice a repeating pattern that flows throughout the book: where the gospel is preached, the Holy Spirit moves people to believe, the church grows, persecution against believers rises, and God intervenes to protect the church.

UNDERSTANDING
THE GOSPELS LITERARILY

Throughout the Gospels, Jesus speaks! What an extraordinarily normal activity for the King of kings, that He would speak to His rebellious ones, His faithful ones, His betrayers. Our Lord came to earth in human flesh to live among us so we might be partakers of His kingdom. Surely if we hear His words in the pages of Scripture, we should pay attention. We know that all the Scriptures are the Word of God and all of them carry power and authority. But it is still a marvel to see Jesus' own incarnated words written down in Scripture for us. Jesus speaks privately to individuals like Nicodemus or the woman at the well. He speaks to small groups of His disciples, explaining parables and teaching them about all that He and they would suffer. He speaks to crowds on mountaintops and on the shore of the sea, proclaiming the good news of His gospel.

NARRATIVES

The content of the Gospels and Acts, like most of the Bible, was shared orally before it was written. Think of the Gospels and Acts more like campfire stories and less like a chronology or linear story you might find in a book. Each story is a self-contained unit. We call any excerpt or passage of Scripture that fits together as a unit a *pericope*. In a narrative, the plot delineates the pericope. The bulk of the Gospels and Acts comprises narrative material, so to decide which verses to include in a pericope, pay attention to the plot, scene and topic changes, and time references.

We can use Luke 6:1-6 as an example:

> *¹On a Sabbath, while he was going through the grainfields, his disciples plucked and ate some heads of grain, rubbing them in their hands. ²But some of the Pharisees said, "Why*

are you doing what is not lawful to do on the Sabbath?"
³And Jesus answered them, "Have you not read what David
did when he was hungry, he and those who were with him:
⁴how he entered the house of God and took and ate the bread
of the Presence, which is not lawful for any but the priests
to eat, and also gave it to those with him?" ⁵And he said to
them, "The Son of Man is lord of the Sabbath."
  ⁶On another Sabbath, he entered the synagogue and was
teaching, and a man was there whose right hand was with-
ered.

The passage opens with "On a Sabbath, while he was going through the grainfields." Then down in verse 6 it says, "On another Sabbath, he entered the synagogue and was teaching." The time references and location changes indicate that verse six begins a new pericope. The end of verse 5, "The Son of Man is lord of the Sabbath," concludes the theme of the previous verses. Sometimes in the middle of a story or parable a smaller pericope explains or serves as the key to understanding the larger pericope. We call these interruptions to a narrative "Markan sandwiches" because they exist primarily in the book of Mark.³ An example of a Markan sandwich would be the story of the healing of Jairus's daughter in Mark 5:21–24, 35–43. This story is interrupted by the hemorrhaging woman touching Jesus' garments (Mark 5:25–34). The faith of this woman becomes an object lesson for Jairus and those from his household whose faith wavered as they wept over the girl's apparent death and who laughed at Jesus' assertion that the girl was sleeping. Jesus healed in response to both strong and weak faith.

Since the Gospels are all about Jesus, we must understand

how to approach biographical details about Jesus' life and ministry. Notice that most of the biographical detail serves to highlight aspects of Jesus' earthly mission: he was born in fulfillment of prophecy "king of the Jews" (Matthew 2:1–12); He was rejected by those in His hometown who should have known and loved Him (Matthew 13:53–58); He taught in the synagogue even as a young boy, and those who heard Him were amazed by His understanding and answers (Luke 2:41–52). As Jesus' life and ministry unfolded, His audiences were His devoted disciples, legalistic religious leaders, power-hungry political leaders, and curious crowds. Consider, as you read biographical sketches about Jesus, His actions, His purpose, and His audience, and their responses.

PARABLES

A parable is a short story that teaches a lesson through allegories and comparisons. At its most basic level, a parable is veiled, symbolic storytelling. In the New Testament, parables are used only by Jesus. Sometimes a parable is highly allegorical, meaning most of the details in the story symbolize other things, such as the parable of the sower (Matthew 13:3–9, 18–23). At other times, a parable compares two things in highly figurative ways, such as many of the "kingdom of God" parables (Matthew 22:1–14, Luke 13:18–21).

In Mark 4:1–12, Jesus began teaching the crowds, mostly through parables. When the disciples and others around Him asked about the parables, He explained that the mystery of the kingdom of God had been given to them. Paul explains that believers receive this hidden mystery as "Christ in you, the hope of glory" (Colossians 1:25–27). The mystery of the kingdom of God that Jesus spoke so frequently about in the Gospels is the fulfillment of all that was anticipated throughout the Old Testament, that the Promised One would come to deliver and restore God's people. The kingdom of God is more than a realm; it is a relationship with the Redeemer and Ruler of humanity. But for those outside the kingdom of God, the kingdom of God remains secret (Mark 4:11), and the message of the parables serves as an indictment against them. Therefore, these outsiders see and don't perceive, hear and don't understand (Mark 4:12). Jesus wanted His followers to understand the parables; that's why He explained them. He didn't expect outsiders to understand so He rarely explained the parables publicly, but only privately (Mark 4:33–34).

To understand parables literarily, treat them like other narratives by identifying the setting, characters, and plot. Pay attention to scene changes and movements within the story, as well as characters' descriptions and the audience's response. Read the parable several times to understand what the characters or elements in the story represent. Sometimes Jesus explains the meaning of the elements in the parable and the parable itself, such as in the parable of the sower (Mark 4:3–20). Finally, look for themes that emerge from the parable, and the lesson the parable is teaching both for the original audience and for our contemporary context.

DIALOGUE

To understand the dialogues of Jesus in the Gospels and of the apostles in Acts literarily, identify the conversation partners. For example, Jesus' conversation partner is Nicodemus in John 3. Second, determine what the dialogue is about. Nicodemus comes to Jesus at night, wanting to learn more from this great teacher (John 3:1–2). Third, consider questions asked or problems to be solved. In this passage, Jesus takes Nicodemus's curiosity to another level by explaining that to see the kingdom of God, one must be born again (John 3:3). Nicodemus, rightfully confused by this statement, asks, "How can a man be born when he is old? Can he enter a second time into his mother's womb and be born?" (John 3:4). Fourth, note Jesus' answers. Jesus gives Nicodemus a long response that I'm pretty sure Nicodemus was not ready for. Jesus tells Nicodemus of the salvation that could be his, explaining that being born again is a spiritual matter. To be spiritually reborn and gain eternal life, one must believe in the Son of God (John 3:5, 16–18). Fifth, note any responses from the conversation partner. In this passage, we don't immediately see Nicodemus's response, but we do see him appear a couple of times later (John 7:50–51; 19:39), which begs the question of whether Nicodemus responded in faith to the message of Christ. This dangling question begs us to ponder whether we will respond in faith to Christ's message.

SPEECHES AND SERMONS

It's easy to get a little overwhelmed when studying Jesus' speeches and sermons because many of them are long and contain lots of smaller pericopes that may blur the big picture. Therefore, consider prayerfully how the part fits into the whole of what Jesus is saying. Take the Sermon on the Mount, which spans three chapters in the book of Matthew (chapters 5 through 7). It starts with a series of poetic blessings that we refer to as the Beatitudes, then moves on to topics like anger, divorce, the treatment of enemies, care for the poor, fasting, and judging others. Interspersed throughout are vivid metaphors, such as "You are the light of the world" (Matthew 5:14), proverbial statements like "For if you forgive others their trespasses, your heavenly Father will also forgive you" (Matthew 6:14), and prayers (Matthew 6:9–13). That is one big sermon!

In the book of Matthew alone, there are five long speeches of Jesus called discourses. All the Gospels contain speeches and sermons, mostly by Jesus, and the book of Acts contains several sermons from the likes of Peter, Stephen, and Paul. To understand these speeches literarily, first look at them as a whole. Read an entire discourse or sermon several times and then read the beginning and end to see if there are bookends that might provide a clue about how the entire speech or sermon holds together. Note any repetitions of words, phrases, or themes. These observations provide a clue to the overall message of the speech or sermon.

Our journey through the metanarrative of Scripture comes to its dramatic climax in Jesus' life, death, resurrection, and ascension. He is the Easter story as He fulfills all of God's instructions in the law. He is the end to which history is pointing. He is the One to whom the poets sing, the One from whom we receive wisdom and understanding, and the One whom the prophets foretold.

TRANSFORM YOUR STUDY OF THE GOSPELS

1. Read the narrative of Luke 6:1–6.

   - Identify the setting, characters, and plot.
   - What is the problem to solve or the question to answer?
   - How does Jesus respond?
   - What is Jesus teaching the Pharisees and disciples about Himself?
   - Given that what Jesus says about Himself is true, how should those who hear Him respond?

2. Read the parable of Matthew 25:1–13.

   - Identify the setting, characters, and other important elements from the parable.
   - Make a list of the elements in the parable and what they represent.
   - What two types of people are being compared? Compare and contrast them.
   - What is this parable actually about?
   - In one or two words, what is the main lesson from this parable?
   - As a believer, how should you respond to the message of this parable?

3. Read the Sermon on the Mount found in Matthew 5–7. It should take about fifteen minutes.

   - Now read chapter 5:1–2 and chapter 7:28–29. Based on these verses alone, what do you think was Jesus' purpose in giving this sermon?

- Read chapter 5:3–12. What repetition of words or themes do you see?
- In one sentence, what is the message Jesus is communicating through the Beatitudes?
- Read Matthew 5:13–16. What are the two metaphors described? What do they represent? Based on that, what should mark Christians?
- Read verses 17–19. Why did Christ come?
- Read verses 20–48. In verse 20, Jesus says that to enter the kingdom of heaven, the righteousness of His followers had to exceed the righteousness of the Pharisees. From verses 21–48, for each pericope, make a chart with two columns. In one column, list what they have heard and in the second column, list what Jesus says in response.
- If we follow what Jesus commands in these verses, what does verse 48 conclude?
- The word *mature* in verse 48 recurs in Philippians 3:15, Colossians 1:28, and James 1:4.
- What is that word, and how does it help us understand what Jesus is calling His followers to do?

9

SNAIL MAIL
(Epistles)

To send a letter is a good way to go somewhere
without moving anything but your heart.
PHYLLIS THEROUX

W hen was the last time you received a handwritten, personal letter? It's been a couple of years for me. A friend had committed a year to recovering the lost art of letter writing, each day writing a family member or friend a personal, handwritten letter. It wasn't anything he announced; a letter just showed up at my house. My husband is close friends with him and had received a letter a few weeks before, but since I'm not as close to him, I had not expected a letter. I was surprised and very much touched by his thoughtfulness. As I read my letter, it was evident that he'd taken time to see me, to recall God's grace in my life, to know specifically how to encourage me in the Lord, and to challenge me to live more faithfully as a Christian. And it was a long letter! I couldn't believe someone I rarely talk to face-to-face had so much to say to me in a letter. I'm guessing he used our random personal interactions, conversations he'd had with my husband, and stuff I'd posted on social media (and he's not very active on social media) to understand my joys and struggles and to speak specifically into my life. For this act of intentionality and love, I'm forever grateful. Reflecting on that letter from a couple of years ago got me wondering if the New Testament epistles may have sparked his inspiration and approach to his year-long letter-writing campaign.

WHAT ARE EPISTLES?

Epistles are the New Testament letters. They make up about 35 percent of the New Testament. The epistles were letters written by disciples of Jesus, after His resurrection, to churches or to other disciples to encourage the church or to address concerns that came to the attention of the author of the letter. Sometimes a letter was dictated by the author and penned by a scribe. At other times, the author may have written the letter himself. They were tailored to a specific audience, either a church in a specific city, or an individual, or a group (for example, when Peter addresses "elect exiles"). The New Testament letters are generally categorized into *Pauline epistles* (those written or dictated by the apostle Paul to specific churches or specific pastors) and *general epistles* (those written by others to the church in general and not to a specific church).

The Pauline epistles (Paul's letters) were primarily written for a gentile (not Jewish) audience. As you read these letters, you definitely want to keep the book of Acts bookmarked.

Acts chronicles the conversion and itinerant ministry of the apostle Paul as he travelled to many of the churches we read about in his epistles. All of the churches that received his letters are mentioned in Acts, and were either places where Paul had visited, or longed to visit, at the time of his writing. Reading the book of Acts provides historical context regarding the cities and individuals Paul is mentioning and directly addressing.

The general epistles were primarily written to Jewish believers. They help us to see the ongoing fulfillment of God's promises to His church. The Gospels show us the fulfillment of God's promises to send our Savior. The epistles show us how God's promises to continue building His kingdom is through the church.[1]

The book of Acts will also be helpful to you as you read the general epistles. You can learn about James and Peter (two authors of epistles) and how they became leaders of the early church. You can also discover James and Peter as you read the Gospels, to find out more about the special relationship they had with Jesus. Reading Acts and the Gospels alongside the epistles will provide biographical, historical, and cultural background that will enhance your understanding of these letters.

Let's explore the similarities between the letters in the Bible and the snail-mail letter I received from my friend with the year-long campaign of recovering the lost art of letter-writing. Letters in the Bible work a lot like snail-mail letters. They are both kind of ancient by today's standards but have a similar format that includes an introduction, the body of the letter, and a closing.

The introduction includes the author's name and any coauthors (sometimes with a self-description like *apostle* or *servant*), the recipient of the letter, a greeting (such as "Grace to you and peace from God our Father and the Lord Jesus Christ" in Romans 1:7), and very often words of thanksgiving and an opening prayer (especially in Paul's epistles).

The body makes up the bulk of the letter and often contains the purpose for writing. See the purpose in 1 Corinthians 1:10, for example: "I appeal to you, brothers, by the name of our Lord Jesus Christ, that all of you agree, and that there be no divisions among you, but that you be united in the same mind and the same judgment." The body of the letter often includes encouragements, such as "Beloved, it is a faithful thing you do in all your efforts for these brothers, strangers as they are" (3 John 5). Sometimes the body of a letter includes warnings: "I warn you, as I warned you before, that those who do such things will not inherit the kingdom of God" (Galatians 5:21). Because the writers of the epistles were church leaders and teachers, the body of the letters often contain commands, direct instruction for living as Christ-followers or for solving specific problems. They contain wonderful doctrinal teaching (see the book of Romans, for example). Finally, the body of the letters are personal, containing updates about individuals and churches, and a host of other things.

The epistles often conclude with personal words of encouragement or instruction, mention of future plans, shout-outs and commendations of colleagues and friends, and acknowledgement of a scribe if one was used. Many wrap up with a short benediction, or blessing, like this one from 1 Thessalonians: "Now may the God of peace himself sanctify you completely, and may your whole spirit and soul and body be kept blameless at the coming of our Lord Jesus Christ" (5:23).

Introduction, body, and closing make up a general format,

but there are exceptions. For example, Galatians doesn't include words of thanksgiving or an opening prayer, James doesn't have a closing, and 2 Peter has no final greetings. Just like the various kinds of letters we're used to sending and receiving, the content of the epistles might have a more personal or intimate tone; they may be more formal or casual; they inform, emote, request, command, exhort. This is natural, as letters are shaped for specific readers—a specific audience.

One way the epistles differ from other letters, either ancient ones or contemporary ones, is that they are generally longer, covering multiple topics in one letter. The books of Romans and 1 and 2 Corinthians are good examples of long letters, teaching and exhorting believers on many topics.

The apostle Paul's letters seem especially meant to encourage, instruct, and warn various churches. Some were written while he was in prison; others were written to pastors in young churches. Some cut to the chase and open with direct rebuke or correction: "I am astonished that you are so quickly deserting him who called you in the grace of Christ and are turning to a different gospel" (Galatians 1:6). Others seem more personal and tender: "But since we were torn away from you, bothers, for a short time, in person not in heart, we endeavored the more eagerly and with great desire to see you face to face" (1 Thessalonians 2:17) or "To Timothy, my true child in the faith" (1 Timothy 1:2). Regardless, each letter is tailored to a specific audience, though there is a sense of repeated themes and warnings among some of Paul's letters, such as the warnings against false teaching in Galatians and Colossians, the call to put away the old life of sin and to put on the new self in Ephesians, Colossians, and Romans, and the reminders of the work of the Spirit in the lives of believers found in 1 Corinthians and Romans.

With all the variety we find in epistles, how do we make sense of them? Although there are common themes among Paul's letters and among the general epistles, we should treat each letter as a complete unit to understand the situation that gave rise to the letter, what the author wanted them to know about the impact of Christ's finished work on their lives, and how he expected them to live as a result of this knowledge. The body of the epistles is sometimes divided into two halves. The first half is generally jam-packed with theological truth about who God is, the gift of the Holy Spirit, and Christ's redemptive work. The second half contains a lot of commands to help the believers live in light of the truth, as well as a series of contrasts between the old life that believers are to leave behind and the new life that Christ has called His people to.

Most of the epistles were meant to be read in one sitting to the whole church, as a complete letter, and then circulated among other churches in the same city. This means that the epistles were written for the ear. There is a similar dynamic in churches when pastors preach sermons. A pastor may write a sermon manuscript, but that manuscript is not the same as writing an essay or book. A sermon is written for the hearer, not the reader. I often hear pastors say that it's hard to turn a sermon series into a book because they have to change much of the language to fit the way that an audience engages with the material. I can tell when a book I'm reading is based on a sermon or a series of spoken messages. I can "hear" the pastor's or speaker's voice as I read. There's a kind of cadence to it that mimics the spoken word. This is the intention of the epistles. Though Paul or James or Peter could not physically be in the presence of the people to whom they wrote, the letters echo their voices in a way that made it feel like the authors were speaking, rather than the letter carrier.

Have you ever heard a pastor preach, and you knew immediately what pastor he studied under or was heavily influenced by? Their word choice, voice, tone, and hand gestures mirrored their mentor. My husband was speaking at a conference in Brazil years ago and was assigned a translator who would stand beside him and translate the message into Portuguese for the largely Portuguese audience. This translator was amazing! Every body movement, gesture, and word my husband made or spoke, the translator mimicked. He wanted the audience to hear and experience the message in Portuguese with the same emotion, tone, and emphasis as my husband. The Roman first-century writer Seneca said that his letters "should be just what my conversation would be if you and I were sitting in one another's company or taking walks together."[2] This is the sense I get with the epistles. The authors wanted the words and tone and emphasis of their letter to carry through to the listeners.

UNDERSTANDING
EPISTLES LITERARILY

Literarily, there are several things we can look out for as we read epistles. First, be sure to connect the context to the person or church that the letter was written to. For example, in Titus, it's important to take note of Crete and why Paul was sending Titus there. The opening chapter also provides a clue about the kind of people the Cretans were: "One of the Cretans, a prophet of their own, said, 'Cretan are always liars, evil beasts, lazy gluttons.' This testimony is true" (Titus 1:12–13). This fairly harsh word comes with the explanation for why sound doctrine would be a key element of the success of the church there: "Therefore rebuke them sharply, that they may be sound in the faith" (1:13).

Another contextual element to consider is the many quotes and allusions to the Old Testament that we find in the epistles. Remember that the Old Testament books were the only Bible the early church had, so throughout the epistles you will find many quotes from and allusions to the Old Testament. Spend some time looking up those Old Testament references to discern how they shed light on the passage.

Second, pay attention to the basic structure of the letter as we mentioned earlier—the introduction, body, and closing—to find helpful contextual information that gives insight into the situations that might be addressed in the letter. We just saw this in the letter to Titus, but even in a book like Hebrews that doesn't follow the pattern of a standard introduction, chapter 1 opens by reminding the audience that God speaks to us through His Son. It goes on to give us a beautiful picture of the supremacy of Christ. Chapter 2 opens with a word of exhortation to believers to pay attention to what they have heard about Christ so that they do not drift away and neglect the great salvation Christ has offered to them. These opening chapters serve as an extended introduction and prologue for the entire book.

Third, ask what the author is doing in the passage. Generally he will either be explaining a theological truth or exhorting believers to right living in light of the truth. Explanations are often statements of fact, which we called *indicatives*. These topics explain key doctrines such as salvation, Christ's redemption or return, or the human condition. Exhortations are commands, which we call *imperatives*. They are the Christian's response to the truth they know.

Fourth, look for where a sentence or paragraph begins and ends to form a unit of thought. In the original manuscripts of the Bible, there were no verse breaks or punctuation. The punctuation has been given to us by the translators of our Bibles. So don't rely conclusively on that. Rather, look for clues in the text that help you to know what ideas go together as a sentence or paragraph. An easy way to do that is to look for repetitions that seem important in a section, connections between words and phrases (often words like *so that, therefore, because, according to*), the overall development of thought from beginning to end, and transition words that provide a clue that a section or topic has ended. Sometimes these clues help you realize a thought is being expounded further ("If then you have been raised with Christ, seek the things that are above" in Colossians 3:1) or a new topic is being picked up ("First of all, then, I urge that supplications, prayers, intercessions, and thanksgivings be made for all people" in 1 Timothy 2:1). You should also pay attention to lists in epistles. Those lists can be vice-and-virtue commands, moral commands, or a string of exhortations. You will most often see them clustered together in a paragraph, sentence, or chapter.

Fifth, sometimes in the epistles, parts of the letter are specific responses to sets of questions or issues that have been brought to the attention of the author of the letter. The book of 1 Corinthians is a good example where we read repeatedly, "Now concerning." The second half of the letter seems to be largely devoted to addressing issues of concern that had been brought to Paul. It's like Jeopardy. We have the answers given in the letter, so our task is to figure out the original questions. Sometimes we get a big hint like, "Now concerning food offered to idols" (1 Corinthians 8:1). This lets us know that the issue Paul was addressing had to do with eating food that had been used as an offering to idols. While we don't know the details of the particular idols or the type of food, we come to understand why this question had been posed to him, how he interpreted the law in light of Christ, and how the believers were expected to conduct themselves among other followers of Christ whose consciences were weak in this area. In other cases, the original question is less clear, but we can make good assumptions based on the literary context of the passage.

Sixth, keep in mind that most often the author of an epistle is making an argument that follows conventional principles of logic. If you were ever given the writing assignment of a persuasive essay, you may be familiar with these elements of laying out an argument. Those elements are:

Claim: What you are trying to prove

Warrant: What informs your thinking about your claim

Proof: Evidence, or examples used to convince your audience

Objections: Potential points of disagreement or disapproval of your claim by opponents

Conclusion: Summary, or applications to leave with your audience

Once you have worked through the passage in this way, paying attention to particular literary elements, the context of the original audience, theological truths and any commands that flow from them, you will have a pretty good idea of what that passage may have meant to first-century believers. Since they and we are living in the fulfillment of God's promises to Israel, whom we learn in the epistles is the church (Romans 2:28–29; 11:11–24; Galatians 3:23–29), you will notice many parallels and intersections between issues that the church faced in the first century and issues we face today (legalism, sexual immorality, false teaching, suffering, personal disputes, doctrinal issues, spiritual gifts, questions surrounding Christ's return). At the same time, you will also notice clear distinctions between their day and ours, like the issue of eating food sacrificed to idols (1 Corinthians 8) or what to do with a runaway slave (Philemon). Identify the similarities and differences to uncover what the passage teaches us about how we live as the people of God redeemed by Christ.

TRANSFORM YOUR STUDY OF EPISTLES

1. Read the book of Philippians at least three times. You may want to combine reading and listening on audio.

2. Take note of the basic structure of the letter. Print out the letter so you can mark the various components:

   • introduction (sender, receiver, coauthors, greeting, prayer)
   • the body (explanations, exhortations, contrasting ideas, instructions)
   • closing (shout-outs, future plans, encouragements, benediction).

3. Now read Philippians 2:12–18.

   • Reread Philippians 2:1–17. How does the word *therefore* in verse 12 connect the preceding verses to the passage of verses 12–18?
   • Read Philippians 2:19–30. How do the examples of Timothy and Epaphroditus connect to verses 12–18?
   • Identify any indicative (teaching points) and imperative (commands) sections, where you find them, and how they are connected.
   • Isolate the main verbs, and mark the beginning and end of a sentence or thought or topic. Pay attention to key words, repetitions, connecting words, and transitional phrases.
   • Identify the main principle from verses 12–18.
   • What other places in Scripture echo this principle?

- What does Jesus say about the main principle you have discovered, or what does He do that embodies this principle?
- How might you walk out that principle in your life? Be specific.

10

THE SCARY STUFF
(Apocalyptic)

Behold, he is coming with the clouds, and every eye will see him,
even those who pierced him, and all tribes of the earth
will wail on account of him. Even so. Amen.

REVELATION 1:7

We all sat nervously in a circle, waiting for someone to start the discussion none of us felt ready for. We had spent weeks preparing, and now we were there, spending a weekend together studying none other than the book of Revelation. I had been leading Bible studies for years and had never led a group through this book of the Bible, so I was nervous as well and trying to shake it off so we could get going. As our first session started, women were shy about sharing what they'd learned, not sure if their contextual work was accurate, and not confident that they were understanding all the imagery. We also realized that seemingly every verse had some biblical connection elsewhere in Scripture, so trying to chase down so many references was daunting and mostly unnecessary for ascertaining the main idea of the passage.

I won't lie. Our first session was rough, but our hearts were filled as we learned together session after session. It didn't take long for us to get into a groove of questioning each other about how we developed our outlines, or how we found the main idea of a passage, or even how we would teach it. Our nervous energy had worn off and been replaced with marvel at our growing understanding of this amazing book. At the end of the weekend, in preparation for our last session together, someone read Revelation 21:1–8. As I looked up from the reading, I noticed women in tears. In more than twenty years of leading Bible studies, this had never happened before, that the reading of God's Word would elicit such emotion from every participant. I'm sure some were probably celebratory tears because we made it through the study. There were also tears of relief, because of the weight of the task we had undertaken, and that it was finally over. But mostly our tears were tears of joyful anticipation. We caught glimpses of the future we Christians long for—for the new heaven and new earth where we will live in God's presence, experiencing His mercy, satisfied by His pleasures forever with no fear of judgment or death.

This is the joy and excitement of apocalyptic literature! While they do contain frightening or confusing elements, the content points our attention to our future hope. The people of God "shall be delivered, everyone whose name shall be found written in the book" (Daniel 12:1). Not only will we be delivered, but God will dwell with us and be with us as our God. He will wipe away every tear, death will be no more nor will there be any mourning or crying or pain ever again (Revelation 21:3–4). Oh, for that day!

WHAT IS APOCALYPTIC LITERATURE?

The key "to enjoying the apocalyptic passages in the Bible is letting go of our realistic inclinations and setting our imaginations free to soar."[1] In the apocalyptic genre, individuals receive divine revelations from God about things that are to come. The term *apocalypse* comes from a Greek word that means "revelation," and that's where the Book of Revelation gets its name. Revelation and the latter half of Daniel are the primary apocalyptic books, but apocalyptic passages appear throughout the Bible—in Zechariah, Matthew, Thessalonians, and Peter, to name a few.

Apocalyptic literature encompasses discussions of eschatology (ES-kuh-TAH-luh-gee), which is the study of the last days. The last days are the time we are living in now, between Christ's first coming and His future return. Generally when people refer to the last days or the end times, they are reflecting Jesus' teaching in Matthew 24. Jesus was asked by one of His disciples, "When will these things be [referring to the destruction of the temple], and what will be the sign of your coming and of the end of the age?" (24:3). Jesus' lengthy response opens what is known as the Olivet Discourse. In this warning passage, Jesus says there will be false Christs, "wars and rumors of wars," persecution of believers, false prophets, and "the abomination of desolation" (possibly referring to the destruction of the temple that would occur in 70 AD, or a future event not disclosed).[2]

As you study apocalyptic books, first take your time. You will want to read chapters several times to get a handle on what's happening. Second, start with the book of Daniel. It will ease you into the apocalyptic genre, and it will help you later when you do get to Revelation, which includes many allusions to Daniel. Third, use the opening chapters as your on-ramp. They provide a lot of context for later chapters, and, compared to the bulk of the visions in each book, they are relatively easy to follow. Fourth, pay attention to the interpretations given in the text. If the writer provides them, great! In both Daniel and Revelation, the first visions are interpreted for you, at least on a basic level. For example, when Daniel sees the vision of the four beasts (Daniel 7:1–8), an angelic being tells him what the beasts symbolize (Daniel 7:15–27). Fifth, stay out of the weeds! Grab the big picture and fill in the gaps later. Don't start off by trying to decipher every image and detail or trying to make sense of all the dates and numbers. Keep your study real basic, like who's doing what to whom and why, and be sure to note the writer's responses to what he's seen.

UNDERSTANDING APOCALYPTIC LITERATURE LITERARILY

Imagery and symbolism are the two main literary features of apocalyptic literature. Try to make sense of them by determining what is actually happening in the text, what it might refer to in the historical context of the original audience, and how it might correspond to our context today.[3] Keep in mind that just about everything is symbolic (except for the bits of narrative interspersed here and there), including objects, people, dates, and creatures. In fact, the creatures are reminiscent of the fantasy genre, with multi-headed beasts, dragons, and an otherworld-like setting.[4]

DANIEL

We put the book of Daniel in the apocalyptic genre, but the first half of the book is narrative. It sets the stage for the latter half through visions given to various kings, which God helps Daniel to interpret. The interpretations of each king's dream center on God's sovereignty over kings and kingdoms to such an extent that the kings all acknowledged that God's kingdom and His rule are forever (Daniel 4:3, 34; 6:26). Daniel's character and God's protection of him are also prominent in the first half of the book. We see that God is faithful to preserve His remnant and deals righteously with all. A big shift occurs in the second half of the book of Daniel as the apocalyptic visions take up most of chapters seven through twelve. They show where the world is headed, that those who oppose God will be held in "shame and everlasting contempt" (Daniel 12:2), but God's people will be saved. The goal is not to scare people but to give God's faithful ones hope as they wait.

Literarily, the apocalyptic visions in Daniel are mostly simile and metaphor. Remember that a simile compares two unrelated things using the words *like* or *as* in the comparison. When Daniel sees the vision of the beasts in chapter 7, the similes help to clarify what he saw. The first beast was *like* a lion, the second beast was *like* a bear, and the third was *like* a leopard (Daniel 7:2–8). The fourth beast was so terrifying Daniel couldn't even compare it to anything else in existence, so no simile is used. When the angel interpreted the vision for Daniel, he turned to metaphors. You will recall that a metaphor compares two unrelated things by calling it something that it is not but relating the two in a meaningful way. Even though the angel says that the beasts *are* four kings, we know that is not actually true, but now we know what they symbolize. The angel goes on to say which kingdom is represented by the different beasts (Daniel 7:17–24).

Other visions read more like narratives so you can use the plot arc technique to help you work through the passage. Overall, try to embrace the symbolic language and imagery and keep the big picture in mind.

REVELATION

The whole book centers around the rule and reign of Christ past, present, and future. Indeed, the entire Bible is a revelation, a revealing of Christ, who was once hidden but has now been manifest through the gospel. One day Jesus will fully reveal Himself to all His creation and redeem all who are His. Revelation claims itself as a letter, a prophecy, and an apocalypse. Its title and content are clearly apocalyptic. The prologue (1:1–3) tells us it is a book of *apokalypsis*, or revelation. As a letter, it opens in the standard form of an epistle, with a greeting: "John to the seven churches that are in Asia: Grace to you and peace from him who is and who was and who is to come, and from the seven spirits who are before his throne" (Revelation 1:4). The format of the book contains all the elements of a letter that we considered in chapter 9. The greeting (1:4–8) lets us know it is a letter from John to the seven churches. Then there's the body of the letter (1:9–22:5), as well as a conclusion (22:6–17) and closing (22:18–21). As a prophecy, the opening verses affirm that this is a book of prophecy (1:3; 22:18). Several times throughout the book, John refers to it as "the words of the prophecy of this book" (Revelation 1:3; 22:7, 19).

John greeted seven churches in Asia that would receive his message. Right away, we see the image of Christ coming with the clouds, and John says, "He is coming" (Revelation 1:7). A voice tells him to write what he sees in a book and to send it to seven churches. When he turned to see the voice, suddenly seven golden lampstands appeared with a man standing in the middle of them. He was *like* a son of man. The description of his physical features is all similes. John tried his best to describe this son of man. When this man speaks, we know that it is Jesus because He says that He died but now lives forever, that He holds the keys to Death and Hades, and that He is the first and the last (Revelation 1:17–18). So it is Jesus who commands John to write the things that he sees. Chapters 2 and 3 are pretty straightforward, and chapters 4 and 5 are beautiful and worshipful and celebratory, so the book takes quite an abrupt shift when the seals are opened and a sense of dread begins to loom. As the plight of the world gets worse, the images become much more difficult to decipher, and we have no idea where we are in history. So how do we make progress in understanding this book?

If you began your studies in apocalyptic literature in Daniel, as previously suggested, that will be a help. In Revelation, you'll recognize many allusions to Daniel. For example, the accounts of the son of man in Daniel 7:9–14 and Revelation 1:7–15 are striking in their similarities. Remember that this book is neither chronological nor literal. Allow the literary elements to take center stage. With Revelation, go slow. Read by lumping together related passages. You might study the churches, then read the throne-room chapters together (chapters 4 and 5) or read the seals chapters together (chapters 6 and 7). Initially, just work on getting the big picture of what is happening through the imagery and how the various characters (and creatures) respond, and how we should respond. For example, in Revelation 4, the scene is the throne in heaven. In verses 1–7 we see God seated on His throne and in verses 8–11 we see creatures around the throne. What is happening in this scene is worship. The creatures are giving glory to God and falling down before Him in worship. In this short example, even if we don't get all the imagery, we get the main idea that the central activity of all creation in heaven is the worship of God as He sits and reigns on His throne. This tells me that God is worthy of worship, and we don't have to wait until heaven to worship Him. We can begin now.

In some ways, Revelation surveys the whole Bible, bringing the epic story of God's redemption to a close. All that God promised to Abraham and his descendants, the restoration He promised wayward Israel, the kingdom of God Jesus ushered in and taught the disciples, the ability to see God face to face and not die but live and worship Him eternally, the mortal taking on immortality—all of this comes to ultimate fulfillment in this last book of the Bible.

TRANSFORM YOUR STUDY OF APOCALYPTIC LITERATURE

The ability to understand the imagery and to place events in a historical context will be key to transforming our study of apocalyptic literature.

1. Read Revelation 12:1–17.

2. Who are the main characters?

3. There are three scenes in this chapter, verses 1–6, 7–12, 13–17. Describe what is happening in each scene (use the words in the text) and the result.

4. What is the picture being painted in each scene? In other words, what does each scene represent?

5. In light of what you learn, how might Christians be encouraged or challenged by this passage? How might someone who is not yet a Christian be challenged or encouraged?

11

A WORD ON CONTEXT

To handle the Bible as the word of God, you must honor its context.

H. B. CHARLES JR., ON PASTORING

W e have been exploring the literary genres and have touched on the importance of historical, cultural, and theological context in Bible study. With literary context, the focus is on the actual words of the text, their literary features and structure. Historical context details the historical situation and events of the time. Cultural context explains social practices, attitudes, and values. Theological context looks at the significance of a passage to our understanding of God and His redemptive purposes as they are fulfilled and revealed in Christ. As we read larger portions of our Bibles—whole books and whole genres—more of the Bible's context becomes available to us. We start to see how the context of the original audience informs our understanding of a specific passage. For example, I've encouraged you to read the book of Deuteronomy for historical and cultural context while you read the prophets, since Deuteronomy lays out not only God's instructions but all the promised blessings for obedience and consequences of disobedience. Repeatedly, the prophets are responding to the disobedience of God's people and warning them of the coming consequences. Or, in the New Testament, the book of Acts provides a lot of historical and cultural context for the epistles.

Even within books and smaller passages, you can read the verses and chapters surrounding a passage you are studying to get a sense of the history and culture of the time. Context is important. It helps us grasp the intended meaning that God, through the biblical author, wanted us to gain from the text. This is called *biblical exegesis* (EX-uh-JEE-sis). When we fail to consider the context surrounding a passage or book, we risk importing meaning into the text that is not really intended by the author. This is called *eisegeis* (EYE-suh-JEE-sis).

Let me encourage you when it comes to context! First, historical and cultural context is helpful, especially if we uncover that context within the pages of Scripture. However, context may not be the *most* important thing, especially if we spend so much time digging into unnecessary or extrabiblical context that we miss the main point of a specific passage. This is a common pitfall for eager Bible students, and I've fallen victim to it myself at times. I can go down the rabbit hole of chasing cross references and studying Bible maps and charts and learning about leprous diseases until I lose the main point of a passage—or worse. I can sometimes lose real communion with the Lord in my study. All the fact-finding can quickly derail our study. Let's discipline ourselves to remember that studying the Bible is primarily a spiritual exercise that uses the intellect. It is not primarily an intellectual exercise cloaked in spirituality. I hope that by dealing with a text literarily first, we can discover the proper historical, cultural, and theological elements that not only clarify the meaning of a passage but also help us properly interpret the passage for us today.

Second, Christian community is an under-utilized source for growing in our knowledge of context. When we study in community, we have the resources of the collective wisdom of everyone in our group to point us to portions of Scripture we may be less familiar with. We can ask and answer questions among peers, get instant feedback, and receive encouragement and correction. The Bible has a long oral tradition that relied on the collective memory of God's people to recall God's mighty acts of deliverance, to remember His faithfulness in the past, and to encourage one another to trust in God's promises of salvation, restoration, and renewal.

JUMPING IN TANDEM

A group of young adults from my church recently returned from a skydiving trip. To hear them talk about it, it was an amazing experience and most of them would definitely go again. Since they were all first-time skydivers, they all jumped in tandem—that is, they were all harnessed to an experienced jumper as they dived out of the airplane. My daughter's instructor told her she seemed like a good candidate to get certified to "solo jump." She came home and immediately searched for skydiving lessons so she could one day advance to jumping alone.

Thank you for jumping in tandem with me through the various biblical genres. I am also jumping in tandem with many fellow Bible teachers and mentors I have learned from and grown with over the years. They have trained me to "jump solo," but I love to bring others with me as we grow together in the grace and knowledge of Christ.

My prayer is that you feel more confident in identifying the main genres found in the Bible, that you can articulate key literary features of each genre, that these tools aid you in understanding the Word of God, and that as your understanding grows so does your love for Christ. As you continue to pray, read, and study, I hope that it's easier for you to open your Bible and know where you are in the metanarrative of Scripture and to find delight in the unfolding of God's Word.

ACKNOWLEDGMENTS

The idea for this book came about during the most tumultuous time of my life—in the middle of a global pandemic, amid serious health concerns for my mom, and in a time when I have felt acutely my need for the Holy Spirit's help. And, boy, did He step in! The Lord provided constant love, flexibility, and support from my amazing husband and children. Thank you, Thabiti, Afiya, Eden, and Titus. God provided food and practical care through my Anacostia River Church family. He gave me the most eager and gifted small group. Thank you, Equipped ladies! God kept me writing and encouraged through my team of prayer warriors and writing cheerleaders and spiritual daughters. Thank you, Ka, Nadia, Mandy, Esi, Ashley, Nicole W., Joani, Kanika, Moira A., Nicole, and Jennifer T. God kept my mom well-cared-for during hospitalizations, surgeries, ER visits, rehab, loads of meds, and doctor visits. Thanks to all the amazing medical staff who have served her. Thank you, Tee Cee and Lee, who put in so many hours and miles caring for my mom. And thanks, Mom, for your love, flexibility, and strength. Thank you, Pastor Greg Hombirg, for opening your church office for me to write during my visits back home. And even though he could never read this book, I'm thankful for my dog, Justice, who provided many opportunities for writing breaks and long walks.

I must also thank my dear friend and acquisitions editor, Trillia Newbell, for your patience, encouragement, and support of this work. This book would not exist without your trust. Thank you, Annette LaPlaca, for your careful edits and suggestions for making my words make sense. Thank you to the entire Moody family for the privilege of working with so many gifted colleagues.

Thank you, Lord, for going before me in so many ways. You keep me writing.

NOTES

CHAPTER 1: AN EPIC STORY

1. The four books about Eragon's adventures comprise Christopher Paolini's *The Inheritance Cycle* (New York: Penguin, Knopf Books for Young Readers, 2012).
2. Gene Roddenberry et al., *Star Trek: The Next Generation*, season 4, episode 25 (California, Paramount Pictures, 2007).
3. Walter A. Elwell and Karry J. Beitzel, "Ahasuerus," *Baker Encyclopedia of the Bible* (Grand Rapids: Baker Book House, 1988), 40.
4. Jonathan Leeman, *The Rule of Love* (Wheaton, IL: Crossway, 2018), 23.
5. Christopher Paolini, *Eragon*, book one of *The Inheritance Cycle* (New York: Penguin, Knopf Books for Young Readers, 2005), 494.

CHAPTER 2: MEANT TO TRANSFORM HEARTS

1. C. S. Lewis, "Sweeter than Honey," *Reflections on the Psalms* (1958) as republished within *C. S. Lewis: Selected Books* (London: HarperCollins, 2002), 310.

CHAPTER 3: RULES, RULES, AND MORE RULES (LAW)

1. Abraham's grandson Jacob was renamed *Israel* after having wrestled with the angel of God. See Genesis 32:22–32.
2. See Jen Wilkins's *Ten Words to Live By: Delighting in and Doing What God Commands* (Wheaton, IL: Crossway Books, 2021).

3. Ligon Duncan, "The Law in the Christian Life," sermon, June 17, 2004. https://ligonduncan.com/the-law-in-the-christian-life-210/.

CHAPTER 4: THIS IS A STORY ALL ABOUT HOW . . . (OLD TESTAMENT NARRATIVE)

1. Sally Lloyd-Jones, "What Stories Do," Ligonier.org blogpost May 1, 2013. https://www.ligonier.org/learn/articles/what-stories-do/.
2. "Yo Home to Bel-Air," DJ Jazzy Jeff & The Fresh Prince, September 21, 1992.
3. Frankie Beverly, "Joy and Pain," recorded by Frankie Beverly and Maze, *Joy and Pain* album (Los Angeles: Capitol Records, 1980).
4. *Ahasuerus* is the king's Aramaic name, pronounced ah-HAHS-veh-ruhsh in Hebrew and commonly pronounced ah-Hah-soo-her-us in English. His Greek name is *Xerxes* (ZERK-seez).
5. Precept Ministries International, *New Inductive Study Bible ESV* (Eugene, OR: Harvest House Publishers, 2013), 836. Also, Walter A. Elwell and Barry J. Beitzel, "Ahasuerus," *Baker Encyclopedia of the Bible* (Grand Rapids: Baker Book House, 1988), 40.
6. When the king asked, "According to the law, what must be done to Queen Vashti" (Esther 1:15), Memucan did not respond, "According to the law," but out of concern that other wives, by Vashti's example, might stand up to their husbands. It's also difficult to tell what "law" the king referred to. As a pagan king who was not a follower of Yahweh, he was certainly not referring to the law of God.

CHAPTER 5: PRAYERS AND SONGS (POETRY)

1. You can find the whole poem "Mr. Nobody" online: Poetry Foundation.org, https://www.poetryfoundation.org/poems/42914/mr-nobody. Accessed September 6, 2021.
2. Edmund Vance Cooke, "Rags," AllPoetry.com, https://allpoetry.com/poem/8619985-Rags-by-Edmund-Vance-Cooke. Accessed September 6, 2021.
3. Mark Vroegop, "Lament Psalms Are a Gift," markvroegop.com, http://markvroegop.com/lament-psalms-are-a-gift/. Pastor Mark Vroegop has written extensively on lament in *Dark Clouds, Deep Mercy: Discovering the Grace of Lament* (Wheaton, IL: Crossway Books, 2019).

4. C. S. Lewis, "Sweeter than Honey," *Reflections on the Psalms* (1958) as republished within *C. S. Lewis: Selected Books* (London: HarperCollins, 2002), 310.

5. The word *stanza* is Italian in origin. There is much debate about the difference between strophe and stanza. Some commentators use the terms interchangeably; others have written entire literary volumes without mentioning either term. I have attempted to create helpful and clear distinctions between the terms and how they can be identified in Scripture. My primary source for understanding the distinctions and functions of strophe and stanza in poetic literature is Mark D. Futato, *Interpreting the Psalms: An Exegetical Handbook* (Grand Rapids: Kregel Academic, 2007), 144.

6. For more on understanding parallelism, see Tremper Longman III, *How to Read the Psalms* (Downers Grove, IL: IVP Academic, InterVarsity Press, 1988), 95–110.

7. Janette Ikz, "Run Ablaze . . . ," *His Testimonies, My Heritage: Women of Color on the Word of God* (Epsom, Surrey, England: The Good Book Company, 2019), 61–62. Used by permission.

CHAPTER 6: A WORD FROM THE WISE (WISDOM)

1. Rev. Edward W. Clayborn, "Your Enemy Cannot Harm You," Rockol, https://www.rockol.com/uk/lyrics-112571502/rev-edward-w-clayborn-your-enemy-cannot-harm-you.

CHAPTER 7: VISIONS OF THE FUTURE (PROPHECY)

1. Gary V. Smith, *Interpreting the Prophetic Books: An Exegetical Handbook* (Grand Rapids: Kregel Academic, 2014), 57.

2. Leland Ryken, "Symbols and Reality: A Guided Study of Prophecy, Apocalypse, and Visionary Literature," *Reading the Bible as Literature* (Bellingham, WA: Lexham Press, 2016), 28.

3. Tremper Longman III, *How to Read the Psalms* (Downers Grove, IL: IVP Academic, InterVarsity Press, 1988), 92.

4. The various oracles are assigned in broad categories to make it easier to remember to look for during Bible study. Many of these categories are taken from Gary V. Smith, *Interpreting the Prophetic Books: An Exegetical Handbook* (Grand Rapids: Kregel Academic, 2014),

and Gordon Fee and Douglas Stuart, *How to Read the Bible for All Its Worth*, 4th ed. (Grand Rapids: Zondervan, 2014).

5. Gordon Fee and Douglas Stuart, *How to Read the Bible for All Its Worth*, 4th ed. (Grand Rapids: Zondervan, 2014), 193.

6. Visions will be covered in chapter 6.

7. Each chapter in Lamentations forms an acrostic poem (except chapter 5). In an acrostic, each verse or set of verses appear in alphabetical order by their first letters. In the Old Testament, they correspond to the twenty-two letters of the Hebrew alphabet. In Lamentations 3, there are three verses for each Hebrew letter. For example, Lamentations 3:1–3 begins with the letter *aleph*.

CHAPTER 8: THE GOOD NEWS (GOSPELS)

1. Anirudh, "Ten Major Accomplishments of Muhammad Ali," Learnodo Newtonic, May 1, 2019. https://learnodo-newtonic.com/muhammad-ali-accomplishments.

2. David Haye, interviewed on CNN June 4, 2016. https://www.youtube.com/watch?v=xbMt6mgkCPU&feature=youtube.

3. James R. Edwards, "Markan Sandwiches: The Significance of Interpolations in Markan Narratives," *Novum Testamentum* 31(3), 1, 1989, 93. https://www.jstor.org/stable/1560460?origin=crossref. Accessed September 6, 2021.

CHAPTER 9: SNAIL MAIL (EPISTLES)

1. John D. Harvey, *Interpreting the General Letters: An Exegetical Handbook* (Grand Rapids: Kregel Academic, 2013), 110–113.

2. Leland Ryken, "Letters of Grace & Beauty: A Guided Literary Study of New Testament Epistles," *Reading the Bible as Literature* (Bellingham, WA: Lexham Press, 2016), 21.

CHAPTER 10: THE SCARY STUFF (APOCALYPTIC)

1. Leland Ryken, "Symbols and Reality: A Guided Study of Prophecy, Apocalypse, and Visionary Literature," *Reading the Bible as Literature* (Bellingham, WA: Lexham Press, 2016), 93.

2. Richard T. France, "Matthew," *New Bible Commentary: 21*st *Century Edition* (Downers Grove, IL: InterVarsity Press, 1994), 936.

3. Duvall J. Scott and J. Daniel Hays, *Grasping God's Word: A Hands-on Approach to Reading, Interpreting, and Applying the Bible* (Grand Rapids: Zondervan, 2012), 320.

4. Gordon Fee and Douglas K. Stuart, *How to Read the Bible for All Its Worth*, 4th ed. (Grand Rapids: Zondervan, 2014), 260–61.

REFLECTION NOTES

_____

_____

_____

_____

_____

_____

_____

_____

_____

_____

_____

_____

_____

_____

The Crete Collective

GROWING CHURCHES IN COMMUNITIES OF COLOR

The Crete Collective exists to start new and to strengthen existing gospel churches in distressed and neglected Black and Brown communities.

We believe the Great Commission requires the church to reach all communities, no matter their social, economic, and ethnic makeup. However, special attention is needed to reach communities of people often invisible, overlooked, marginalized, or neglected.

The Crete Collective series of books seeks to help the church reach communities least engaged with fresh gospel ministry. We aim to provide biblical, readable, relevant, and culturally aware resources written by, for, or about Black and Brown communities.

To find out more about The Crete Collective and to support our mission, visit us at **TheCreteCollective.org** or follow us **@CreteCollective**.